Finishing
Techniques
for
Hand Knitters

Finishing
Techniques
for
Hand Knitters

JANE CROWFOOT

Search Press

A QUARTO BOOK

Published in 2003 by Search Press Ltd
Wellwood
North Farm Road
Tunbridge Wells
Kent TN2 3DR
United Kingdom

Reprinted 2003, 2004 , 2005, 2006, 2008 , 2009

ISBN-10 : 1-903975-84-0
ISBN-13 : 978-1-903975-84-8

A catalogue record for this book is available from the British Library.

QUAR.ASU

Conceived, designed, and produced by
Quarto Publishing plc
The Old Brewery
6 Blundell Street
London N7 9BH

Project Editors: **Tracie Lee Davis, Fiona Robertson**
Senior Art Editor: **Sally Bond**
Designer: **Elizabeth Healey**
Editor: **Sarah Hoggett**
Photographer: **Martin Norris**
Proofreader: **Anne Plume**
Indexer: **Diana Le Core**

Art Director: **Moira Clinch**
Publisher: **Piers Spence**

Manufactured by Universal Graphics Pte Ltd, Singapore
Printed in China by SNP Leefung Printers Trading Ltd

9 8 7

Contents

GETTING STARTED   6

Materials and equipment   8
Basic skills   16

FINISHING TECHNIQUES   28

Shaping techniques   30
Sewn stitches   35
Picking up stitches   44
Casting on and binding
    off techniques   46
Care essentials   56
Additions   58
Buttons and buttonholes   62
Embellishments   68
Correcting mistakes   82
Directory of edgings   86
Color work   92

PROJECTS   100

PATCHWORK CUSHION   102
    Embellished cushion   104
    Intarsia cushion   105
CHILD'S SWEATER   106
    Embroidered sweater with
        picot edge   108
    Boy's sweater with
        intarsia detail   110
WOMAN'S SWEATER WITH
    LACY BORDER   112
    Sweater with Fair Isle border   115
SMALL SHOULDER BAG WITH
    FLAP DETAIL   118
    Drawstring coin bag with
        Fair Isle detail   120
    Beaded handbag   121
MAN'S SWEATER WITH SEED
    STITCH BORDERS   122
    Man's sweater with zipper   124

Index   126
Credits   128

CHAPTER 1

Getting Started

Materials and equipment

At the most basic level, all you need to create a knitted fabric are needles and yarn. As you improve your skills, however, you will soon discover that there is a whole array of materials and equipment at your disposal—from useful gadgets to make your life easier, to items that are used for very specific knitting styles or techniques. This section provides an overview of what is available.

Needles

Historically, knitting needles were made from wood or bone, but today they are usually made from plastic, aluminum, or bamboo. But although the materials may vary, all knitting needles need to be long enough (to hold the width of the fabric being knitted), strong (to hold the weight of the yarn), and smooth (so that the yarn doesn't snag).

Knitting needles come in three main forms. Circular needles—two short needles joined together by a nylon or thin metal cord—allow you to work in the round, using plain, or knit, stitches to create a seamless fabric. The weight of the knitted piece rests on your lap, so this type of needle is particularly useful if you are working with a heavy or bulky yarn. You can buy circular needle tips in a set with one connecting piece, which is screwed on. This enables you to carry around a large selection of needle sizes.

Double-pointed needles come in sets of four or five. Like circular needles, they allow you to work in the round, but they also make it possible to change direction. This is useful when turning the heel on a sock, for example.

In Europe, the most commonly used needles are simply a set of two smooth sticks with an end piece to stop the stitches from falling off.

Needle sizes

Needles come in different diameters as well as lengths so that the knitted stitch achieves the correct gauge for the article being made. Unfortunately, there is no universal guide for knitting needle sizes. There are three main categories: American, metric, and imperial (also known as British).

AMERICAN NEEDLE SIZES

American needle sizes generally range from 0 to 15, with the diameter increasing as the number gets larger. It is also possible to find jumbo sized 17 and 19 needles for knitting very chunky yarn, and needles as small as 0 to 0000 for very fine lace knitting.

METRIC NEEDLE SIZES

Metric needle sizes are the ones most commonly used in Europe. They give the actual diameter of the needle in millimeters, with sizes starting at 2 mm and going up to 20 mm.

U.K. NEEDLE SIZES

The old U.K. needle-sizing system, which is still often used by some knitters, ranges from 14 to 000. It is the opposite of the American system: the higher the number, the smaller the needle.

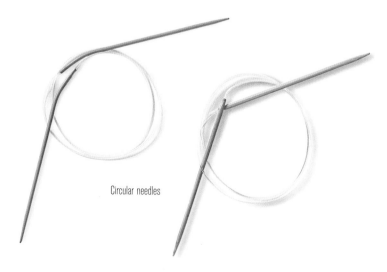

Circular needles

KNITTING NEEDLE SIZES

U.S.	Metric	U.K.
0	2 mm	14
1	2.25 mm	13
	2.5 mm	
2	2.75 mm	12
	3 mm	11
3	3.25 mm	10
4	3.5 mm	
5	3.75 mm	9
6	4 mm	8
7	4.5 mm	7
8	5 mm	6
9	5.5 mm	5
10	6 mm	4
10½	6.5 mm	3
	7 mm	2
	7.5 mm	1
11	8 mm	0
13	9 mm	00
15	10 mm	000

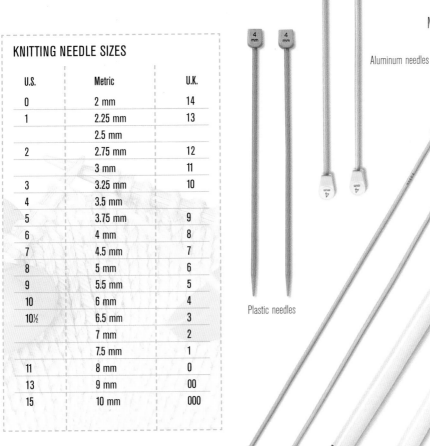

Aluminum needles

Bamboo needles

Jumbo plastic needles

Plastic needles

Needle gauge

Cable needles

Other essential knitting equipment

In addition to knitting needles, there are a few essentials that every knitter should have in his or her workbox.

Needle gauge

Not all needles are marked with a size. A needle gauge has a series of holes running down the center. Push the needle through the holes until you find the one nearest to its diameter.

Cable needles

Cable needles are used to hold stitches while you transfer or cross stitches over from one needle to another for Aran or cable patterns. They are available in different diameters and lengths and conform to the standard knitting-needle size guides although, provided you do not stretch the stitches, you don't have to use the same size needle as you used to knit. Cranked cable needles that have a U-shape at the center eliminate the chance of the stitch slipping, but they can make the knitting process more lengthy.

TIP

When choosing needles, the most important thing is to make sure that the tips are not damaged, or too sharp, or too blunt. Needles should be comfortable to hold and suited to the style of knitting you are doing, so that you enjoy the process, as well as the end result.

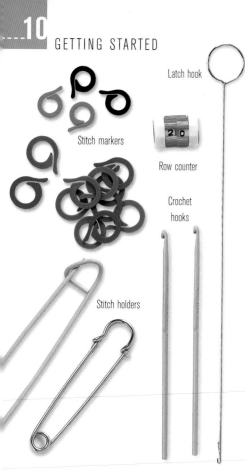

Latch hook

Row counter

Crochet hooks

Stitch markers

Stitch holders

Latch hooks

Similar in appearance to a crochet hook, a latch hook has a fine metal hook at one end with a hinged lever covering it. Latch hooks are also known as rug hooks and are used to pick up or hold dropped stitches.

Stitch markers

Stitch markers are usually brightly colored and made from plastic. They tend to be circular, and look somewhat like a small coil with a split on one side. Stitch markers are used to mark stitch detailing, such as increases and decreases and cable positions. They are also a useful way of marking the beginning of new rows when you are using circular needles or sets of four needles.

Stitch holder

A stitch holder looks like a large safety pin and is used to hold stitches before binding off or adding a detail, such as a neckline, to the work. You can use safety pins instead, but they tend to be sharp and may split the yarn.

Point protectors

Point protectors

Point protectors are made from flexible plastic or rubber, and are like a small tag with two holes for the needles to slip into. As the name suggests, point protectors are used to keep the needle points from becoming damaged, to eliminate the risk of work sliding off the needles, and to protect the knitter from an accidental jab while the piece is in a workbag.

Row counter

A row counter is a small cylinder with a hole running through the center and rotating numbers inside it. You have to remember to turn the dial at the end of every row, since the row counter does not count automatically.

Sewing needles

Knitters' sewing needles are large and blunt and are often sold in packs of two or more. They have different-size eyes to accommodate various plies of yarn. For sewing chunkier knits, you need a ball-ended needle, or bodkin.

Pins

The best pins to use on a knitted fabric are long with brightly colored tips.

Crochet hooks

Available in different sizes, crochet hooks are shorter than knitting needles and are blunt at one end with a U-shaped hook at the other. Crochet hooks can be used to pick up dropped stitches and for a speedy bind-off.

Scissors and tape measure

Small sharp scissors and a good tape measure are essential. The best tape measures for knitters are the retractable dress-making type. It is best to have one marked with both inches and centimeters.

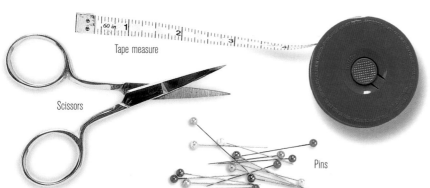

Tape measure

Scissors

Pins

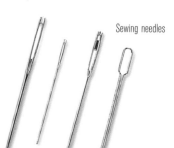

Sewing needles

Additional accessories

When you progress to projects with a higher level of difficulty, you will require a few additional items of equipment.

Bobbins

Graph paper, pencil, eraser, and calculator

Bobbins

For color work, especially intarsia, you may need to wind yarn onto a bobbin to cut down on bulk and tangling on the reverse of the work.

Graph paper

Graph paper is essential to plot motifs or pattern details.

Yarn swift or ball winder

Sometimes yarn is sold in hanks, rather than in a ball, but it has to be wound into a ball before you can start knitting. You can do this by hand, but it is much quicker to use a yarn swift or ball winder.

Bags and baskets

Essential for storing work and equipment.

Pom-pom makers

You can make pom-poms by winding yarn around pieces of cardboard, but plastic pom-pom makers last well and have a groove around them that makes it easier to cut through the yarn.

Knitting spool

A knitting spool (also known as a French knitting doll) is used to make a cord of knitted fabric. Wrap yarn around a series of pegs and then slip the bottom loops over the top ones with a small blunt pin.

Notebook or scrapbook

It is a good idea to make a note of any changes you make to an existing pattern for future reference. Small scrapbooks are handy for jotting down design ideas or storing cuttings from magazines.

Knitting spool

Pom-pom maker

Storage bag

TIPS

Bobby pins are good replacements for knitter's pins as they have great gripping capabilities and are less likely to fall out of the fabric.

Instead of using stitch markers, knot small pieces of yarn in a contrasting color in place.

Longer lengths of yarn can be used instead of stitch holders to hold large numbers of stitches in place.

Yarns

Deciding what type of yarn to use is the most important decision you have to make as a knitter. The finished appearance of the piece can depend entirely on the quality of the yarn, whatever the standard of knitting and finishing. You also need to consider a fiber's suitability for a project: baby clothes, for example, are best made in a soft, easily washable yarn.

Yarn content falls into three main categories: those of animal origin; those of plant origin; and synthetic or man-made yarns.

Yarns of animal origin:

Yarns of animal origin have been in use for thousands of years. The fleeces or threads produced by animals can be spun and then either knitted or woven to produce a fabric. Yarns of animal origin tend to be very versatile in that they can keep you warm when it's cold or cool when the weather is warm.

WOOL, MOHAIR, ALPACA, ANGORA, CASHMERE, AND CAMEL HAIR

Traditionally, the most common knitting yarn has been wool from sheep, but many other animals produce a fleece suitable for spinning yarn. Breeds of goat—such as the angora—which produce mohair and cashmere, are particularly suited to knitting yarn. The hair from alpaca, camels, and angora rabbits can also be spun.

The advantage of wool is that it is warm and strong and is capable of absorbing up to 30% of its own weight in moisture without feeling damp. Wool is easy to dye but can stretch if loosely spun.

Wool

Silk

SILK

A silkworm produces two fine threads from the top of its head that it spins to form a cocoon around itself. The thread produced can be more than 1,600 yards (1,500 m) long. This filament is naturally threadlike and therefore does not need to be spun before being used as a knitting yarn. Silk is available in two qualities: wild, which produces a coarse thread, and cultivated, which creates a finer thread. Both qualities are expensive because of the intensive farming they require. As a knitting yarn, silk can be brittle and has a tendency to stretch.

Yarns of plant origin:

Most yarns of plant origin are produced in warm climates. Cotton is native to the United States, ramie and linen come from the Far East. Yarns of plant origin tend to be cooler than those of animal origin.

COTTON

Cotton has become more popular over the last few years and is a good medium for the hand knitter. It washes well and is cool to wear. It is also a good alternative to yarns of animal origin for people who suffer from allergies. Cotton can be heavy, so it is important to achieve the correct knitted gauge to prevent garments stretching out of shape.

LINEN

Linen is made from the stem of the flax plant; it is very strong and washes well. Like wool, linen absorbs moisture, and so is especially suited to hot climates. Linen can be stiff and is prone to creasing; because of this, yarn manufacturers often mix it with cotton or a light man-made fiber.

Linen

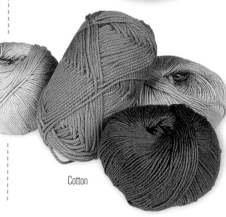

Cotton

Raffia

RAMIE

Ramie originated in China and Japan, but it is beginning to be more widely used. It is very much like linen in appearance and texture, but it is heavier and does not wash particularly well. Like linen, it is often spun with another yarn.

HEMP, JUTE, SISAL, AND RAFFIA

Hemp and jute are fibers produced from the stems of plants of the same name. Sisal comes from the agave plant. Raffia is a type of straw. All these fibers are heavier and coarser than linen and are generally used to make twines, sacking cloth, or burlap, and in basket making.

Synthetic or man-made yarns

Most synthetic fibers are a coal or petroleum derivative. They tend to be cheap since they are easy to produce, and are especially good for allergy sufferers. However, they can be very warm to wear.

NYLON

Nylon was first produced by Dupont in 1938 and revolutionized textile and fiber production.

ACRYLIC AND POLYESTER

Acrylic and polyester are now the most widely used synthetic fibers because they are easy to care for and inexpensive.

RAYON

Rayon is very shiny and takes dye extremely quickly and easily. It is often used to make metallic and colored elastic thread.

Ply

Before they can be used for knitting, most fibers need to be processed in some way to form a yarn. Each strand of fiber is known as a ply, and a yarn is made up of a number of plies spun together.

Obviously the yarn produced can vary greatly in thickness or weight. Traditionally, different terms are used to define different weights of yarn; for example, worsted, DK, sport, and bulky. Today, however, yarns are often produced simply to knit to a certain gauge.

The way in which a fiber is twisted while it is being spun also has an effect on its appearance. The yarn can have an S- or a Z-twist, or it may conform to a yarn structure with a specific name.

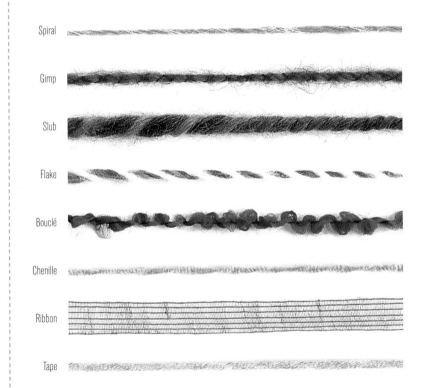

Spiral

Gimp

Slub

Flake

Bouclé

Chenille

Ribbon

Tape

Viscose/polyester mix

Buying yarn

The way that yarns are packaged varies depending on the manufacturer and the type of yarn. Yarn can be bought in a hank, which is a loosely wound coil of yarn twisted around itself; if you buy yarn in a hank, you must unravel it and wind it into a ball before you use it. Yarn also comes as a ready-wound ball, or skein, available in many sizes. In most cases, the yarn can be pulled from the center of the ball to stop the ball from jumping around once knitting is started. Some yarns are sold on cards or cardboard tubes. Cones and spools of yarn tend to be used for machine knitting.

Most yarns sold commercially for knitting come in certain weights—usually 2 or 4 ounces (50 or 100 g), although larger amounts are possible, especially for acrylic-mix yarns, which can be sold in 8-ounce (200-g) balls.

TIPS

If you cannot avoid buying yarns from different dye lots, use odd balls on small areas, such as cuffs, and try to stick to the same dye lot for the main garment pieces, such as the front. If this is not possible, then use the two dye lots simultaneously by working two rows in one and then two rows in another.

Always keep one ball band as a reference. Pin it to the gauge swatch and keep it safe, together with any leftover yarn and spare buttons. This gives you a handy reference for washing instructions and leaves leftover pieces for emergency repairs or alterations.

Ball band information

Regardless of how the yarn is packaged, it usually has a paper band or tag attached to it. This band gives you important information.

The heading on the band shows the company logo, the yarn name and its knitting weight—for example, worsted (also called 4-ply).

The band also tells you what the yarn is made from, and gives you the length of the yarn in the ball. Some bands show a small graph of the recommended knitted gauge (see page 24), washing and pressing requirements (see pages 56–57), the recommended needle size for both knitting and crochet, and the shade and dye lot number. (You must ensure that all the yarn you use for a single project comes from the same dye lot. Slight differences in color could be quite noticable in the knitted piece.) Other bands give recommended gauges—for example, 2.5 stitches per inch on size 10 needles—instead of a graph.

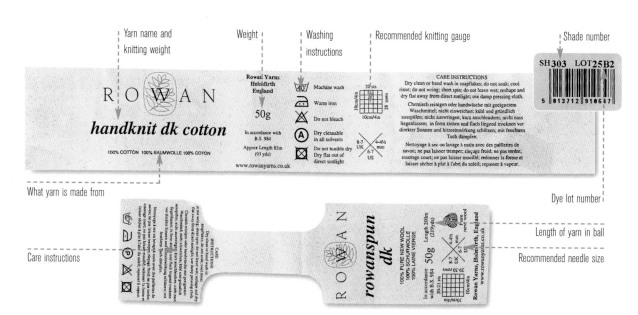

Yarn name and knitting weight

Weight

Washing instructions

Recommended knitting gauge

Shade number

What yarn is made from

Care instructions

Dye lot number

Length of yarn in ball

Recommended needle size

Reading the pattern

Once you've chosen your pattern, you'll want to start knitting as quickly as possible. However, it is very important that you read through the whole pattern before you begin a project.

Most garment knitting patterns are written for more than one size, and these sizes are given on the pattern. The smallest size is shown first, with subsequent sizes in brackets or parentheses. There also should be at least three finished measurements: the chest/bust measurement taken under the arm; the length from the back of the neck to the very bottom edge of the garment; and the sleeve length from the beginning of the cuff to the widest point. There may also be a small schematic drawing showing these measurements and the garment's general shape.

Yarn amounts also appear at the beginning of the pattern. Make sure that you've bought the right yarn and weight or, if you're substituting another quality of yarn, check that the yardage, or meterage, amounts to the same. It is wise to buy a little more than the pattern stipulates.

The pattern tells you what needles you need to achieve the recommended gauge, and whether any additional equipment, such as cable

needles or stitch holders, is required. It also lists the number and size of any buttons and zippers, and any other items that you will need to complete the garment, such as ribbon, elastic, and tapes.

At the beginning of the pattern, you normally find a list of abbreviations and terminology. If you are working from a pattern in a book, there is a list of abbreviations at either the front or the back. Most abbreviations are logical and easy to understand once you're used to them. A list of common abbreviations and their meanings is given on page 27. In this book, an asterisk (*) is sometimes placed in the instructions to indicate the point to which you should return when you reach the phrase "Repeat from *."

Finally, you must knit a gauge swatch before you begin a project (see page 24). The pattern tells you the number of stitches and rows you should have in a 4-inch (10-cm) square. Be sure to use needles that help you get the correct gauge.

This sweater includes an "argyle" motif, which would be difficult to create without following a graph pattern (see page 99)

Basic skills

It is important to be well prepared before you settle down to knit. Make sure that everything you need is close at hand. If possible, sit in a chair with little or no restriction on arm movement and with back support. Comfort is one of the keys to a satisfying knitting experience. Noise and interruptions also need to be kept to a minimum, especially for the novice. Never rush: There is nothing more frustrating than knitting to a deadline, so always allow plenty of time if you're knitting something for a specific occasion (for example, to give as a gift). Stress can also affect the gauge and therefore the overall appearance of the finished piece.

This chapter introduces you to all the basic knitting skills you need to get started. Work through the steps slowly and thoroughly to learn how to hold the needles, cast on stitches, and work various stitch combinations. By doing this you will discover the most comfortable, quickest, and most enjoyable way for you to start knitting.

Scottish or English method

Both needles are held from above. The left hand holds both needles while the stitch is being made, leaving the right hand to make the stitch.

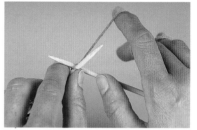

Wrap the yarn around the fingers of your right hand by taking it around the little finger, over the ring finger, under the middle finger, and over the forefinger. Hold the yarn at the back of the work for a knit stitch and at the front for a purl. Use your left hand to move the stitches near the end of the left-hand needle and to guide the right needle into and out of the stitches.

Holding the needles

A knitted fabric is created by working knit and purl stitches after a cast-on row. The way needles are held varies with the knitter. Regardless of whether you are left- or right-handed, try one of the three following techniques.

TIP

Learning to knit successfully relies upon training both hands to create a knitted stitch. If you are left-handed, try to follow the same instructions as for right-handed people. Reversing the process, or learning to knit in front of a mirror, can create problems when you're working from charts and patterns, and is therefore not advisable.

German or continental method

This is considered the fastest way of hand knitting. The yarn is held by the left hand.

Hold both needles as for the Scottish method. Wrap the yarn around your left little finger and over the top of the forefinger. Use the right needle to make the stitch, controlling the gauge with your left hand.

French method

This is considered a more elegant way of knitting than the Scottish method. The only difference is the way the right-hand needle is held.

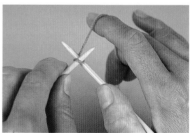

Wrap the yarn around your fingers as for the Scottish method, holding the right-hand needle from underneath as if it were a pencil. Use the forefinger of your right hand to guide the yarn.

Key cast-ons

There are many different ways to cast on, but most have a similar appearance. The key to a good cast-on is an even tension that allows you to work the first row with ease.

Making a slipknot

Most cast-on methods rely on making a first stitch from which subsequent stitches are created. This stitch is best made using a slipknot.

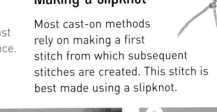

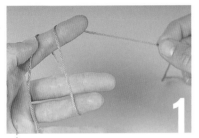

Make a loop in the yarn by wrapping it around the three middle fingers of your left hand in a clockwise direction.

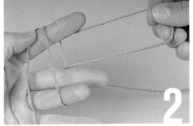

Pass the yarn held in your right hand under the existing loop to form a second loop.

Place this loop on the needle, remove your fingers from the left-hand loop, and pull the yarns to tighten.

Casting on using the thumb method

To cast on using the thumb method, you need two lengths of yarn that are worked simultaneously. The slipknot that forms the first stitch must be far enough along the yarn to create two ends—one free and the other attached to the ball (see the Tip on page 18).

Place the slipknot on the needle and hold the needle in your right hand. *Take the tail end of yarn around your left thumb in a clockwise direction to form a loop.

Slide the needle upward through the loop on your thumb.

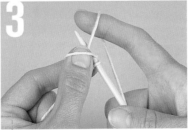

Take the yarn held in your right hand counterclockwise around the needle from back to front.

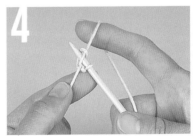

Transfer the loop from your thumb onto the needle and pull the end to tighten. Repeat from*.

Long-tail cast on

This method is also known as the German, or double cable, method.

Place the slipknot on the needle, leaving a long tail, and hold the needle in your right hand. *Wrap the free end of yarn around your left thumb from front to back. Place the other yarn over your left forefinger and hold both threads in the palm of your hand.

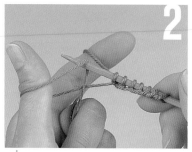

Slide the needle up through the loop on your thumb and over the top of the yarn on your forefinger.

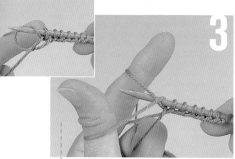

Draw the yarn through the loop on your thumb. Transfer the loop from your thumb to the needle and pull to tighten. Repeat from *.

TIP

To calculate how long the tail end of yarn needs to be when using the thumb or long-tail cast on method of casting on, measure out the yarn to three times the width of the cast-on needed. So, for example, if the width of the knitted piece is to be 4 inches (10 cm), you will need 12 inches (30 cm) of yarn.

This also applies if you are nearing the end of a ball of yarn and are not sure whether there is enough to complete a row.

Casting on with 2 needles using the cable method

This method uses both needles and creates a double edge. It gives a strong cast-on, although it is not quite as "elastic" as the thumb or finger-and-thumb methods.

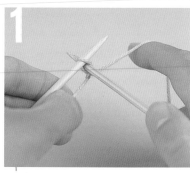

Place the slipknot on the left-hand needle. Slide the right needle upward through the knot from front to back. Take the yarn in your right hand around the right needle in a clockwise direction from back to front.

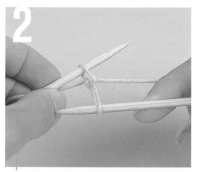

Slide the needle down and back through the knot, catching the wrapped yarn and making a loop on the right needle.

Invisible cast-on

This method is worked on a single rib only. Using a contrasting thread and the cable method, cast on half the number of stitches required. An even number of stitches is needed, so cast on one extra if need be.

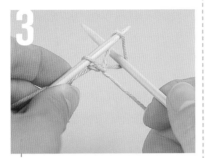

3
Place the left needle under and up through the front of the loop on the right needle. Remove the right needle, thus transferring the stitch onto the left needle.

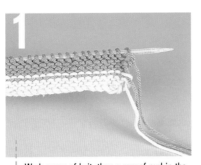

1
Work a row of knit, then a row of purl in the first yarn, then work four subsequent rows of stockinette stitch in the yarn required to complete the knitted piece.

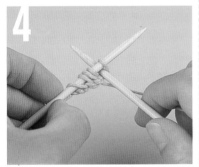

4
To make subsequent stitches, work the same process, but begin by placing the right needle between the first two stitches on the left needle.

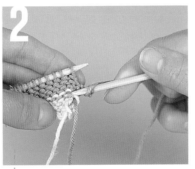

2
On the next row, purl one stitch from the left needle. Using the right needle, pick up a loop in the same color from the row where the contrast yarn finished.

3
Place the loop on the left-hand needle. Take the yarn to the back of the work and knit the stitch.

TIP

When learning to knit, use a light-colored yarn, preferably of pure fiber content so that stitches are easy to see and are not slippery. Yarns high in man-made fiber can be "sticky" and may split easily. Do not use a fashion or specialty yarn such as chenille or anything with a slub or loopy twist, as the stitches will tend to slip or snag.

4
Purl the next stitch on the left needle, then pick up the next loop along from the row where the color changed and repeat from *.

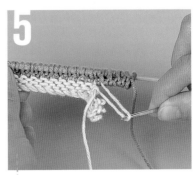

5
When the row is completed, unravel the contrast yarn.

How to produce a knitted fabric

There are two basic knitting stitches—knit and purl. However complicated the finished appearance of the knitted fabric, it will always have been produced using one or both of these stitches.

How to knit a stitch

Cast on the required number of stitches. *Hold the yarn at the back of the work and slide the right needle upward through the first stitch on the left needle from front to back.

Using your right forefinger, take the yarn around the right needle in a counterclockwise direction from back to front.

Slide the right needle down and back through the stitch, making a loop on the right needle. Slip the original stitch off the left needle. Repeat from *.

How to purl a stitch

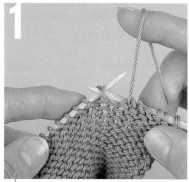  

Cast on the required number of stitches. *Hold the yarn at the front of the work and slide the right needle downward through the first stitch on the left needle from right to left.

Using your right forefinger, take the yarn around the right needle in a counterclockwise direction and back to the front.

Slide the right needle back up through the stitch, catching the yarn to create a loop on the right needle. Slip the original stitch off the left needle. Repeat from *.

German or continental method

If you choose to knit using the German or continental method, the yarn is held in your left hand. Knit and purl stitches therefore are worked in a different way from that previously described.

HOW TO PURL A STITCH

Hold the yarn at the front of the work under your left thumb.

Insert the right needle through the first stitch on the left needle from right to left, over the yarn held by your thumb, thus making a loop around the needle.

HOW TO KNIT A STITCH

Hold the yarn at the back of the work and over your left index finger.

Insert the right needle up through the first stitch from front to back. Take the right needle around behind the yarn on your left finger from right to left.

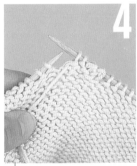

Using the right needle, push the looped yarn backward through the original stitch.

Slip the original stitch from the left needle, leaving the new stitch on the right needle.

Using the right needle, draw the yarn through the center of the stitch on the left needle.

Slip the original stitch from the left needle, leaving the new stitch on the right needle.

Turning the work

At the end of every row, whether it has been a knit or a purl row, you will need to turn the work in order to complete the next row. This means that the left needle becomes empty as the stitches are worked onto the right needle and that the left needle is then transferred to the right hand to begin the next row. In some cases, such as short row shaping, the knitter may be instructed to turn the work part way through a row. In this case simply turn the work around so that the opposite side is facing, and work the row as instructed.

How to slip a stitch

In some techniques the knitter may be required to slip a stitch. In most cases this will mean that a stitch needs to be passed from one needle to another. The way that a stitch is slipped will determine the way that it sits on the needle, so it will need to be slipped either "knitwise" or "purlwise."

To slip a stitch knitwise, insert the right needle into the stitch as if to knit and slip from the left needle. To slip a stitch purlwise, insert the right needle into the stitch as if to purl and slip from the left needle.

Garter stitch

Garter stitch is created by working knit or purl stitches only on every row. It produces quite an "elastic," but dense, fabric.

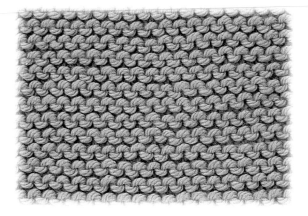

Stockinette stitch

Stockinette stitch is created by working a knit row and then a purl row in repeats. The appearance of this fabric is smooth and flat.

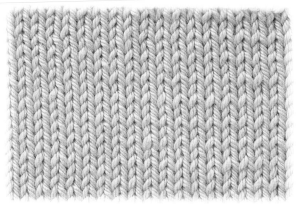

Seed stitch or moss stitch

Seed stitch or moss stitch as it is also known, begins in the same way as a rib in that the rows are made up of alternate knit and purl stitches. On subsequent rows, however, the stitches are worked so that they do not match up to the row below: instead, purl sits on top of knit, and knit on top of purl. It creates a hard-wearing, textured fabric.

Rib

Traditionally, many garments begin with a rib because it keeps the edge of the work tight and can prevent items from becoming misshapen or baggy with use. A rib is created by alternating knit and purl stitches along one row and then, on subsequent rows, matching stitches over the top of each other (so that knit stitches sit on top of knit stitches, and purl on top of purl, and so on). On both sides of the work the stitches line up to form small ridges. Ribs can be regular, such as single rib which is made up of one knit stitch then one purl stitch, or double rib, which is Knit 2, Purl 2. Or they can be irregular, Knit 3, Purl 1 for example.

Double rib

Single rib

The right side and wrong side

In order to continue to knit, you need to be able to differentiate between the appearance of a knit and a purl stitch and the right and the wrong sides of the work.

In garter stitch, both sides of the fabric look the same so the right and wrong side can be determined by the cast-on row or by placing a marker of some kind.

In stockinette stitch, one side of the work is smooth and the other slightly bumpy. If the smooth side is facing you, the next row should be a knit row; if the bumpy side is facing you, then the next row should be purl. Stockinette stitch can also be used on the reverse, known as reverse stitch.

TIPS

Try not to put down a piece in the middle of a row as stitches can become stretched and create an uneven gauge. If this is unavoidable, pick the row back before you start knitting again. (See Unraveling stitch by stitch, page 84.)

If you have left a piece of work for more than a week (sometimes less, depending on the yarn), unravel the last row. Sometimes stitches left on the needle for too long can create a ridge in the fabric.

Garter stitch

Both sides are the same

Stockinette stitch

Right side

Wrong side

Importance of gauge

Before you start a knitted project, it is advisable to work a small swatch to measure the gauge. The gauge is the number of stitches and rows in a 4-inch (10-cm) square: most patterns give an ideal gauge. Cast on a few more stitches and work more rows than the pattern suggests. This way a true gauge is achieved within the square.

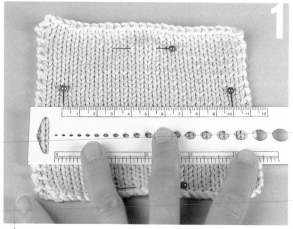

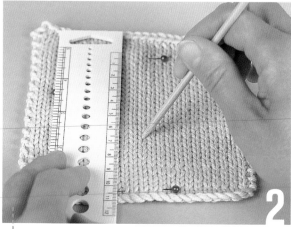

When you've completed the swatch, take a ruler and measure 4 inches (10 cm) across the square and mark with pins. Do the same vertically.

Using the point of a knitting needle, count the number of stitches and rows between the pins.

If you find that you have more rows or stitches than the pattern suggests, then the gauge is too tight and you should switch to a larger needle. If there are fewer stitches or rows, then switch to a smaller size. In some cases, a knitter's gauge may be looser on a purl row than on a knit, creating a fabric containing small ridges. If there is a marked difference in gauge, try changing the needle size for one row of stitching only—for example, use a no. 5 (3.75 mm) needle on a knit row and a no. 4 (3.5 mm) needle on a purl row.

Too tight

Correct gauge

Too loose

Circular knitting

Circular knitting, or knitting in the round, are terms used to describe a method of knitting that creates a seamless fabric made up of knit stitches only. The method can be worked on circular needles or on a set of four double-pointed needles. The oldest surviving pieces of knitted fabric are socks discovered in Egypt dating back to between 1200 and 1500 A.D. The socks have been worked in the round and in places show two colors to a row. Paintings by Italian artists dating back to the mid-1300s depict the Madonna holding knitting arranged on sets of four double-pointed needles.

There are many advantages to working with sets of four or circular needles and they are especially useful when using the Fair Isle technique or working neckbands or cuffs. The only technique that cannot be worked in the round is intarsia.

As with all knitting, work a swatch to judge the gauge, as the gauge can change when using a combination of knit and purl rows.

Circular needles

Make sure the circular needle is long enough to hold the number of stitches in the pattern. Cast on the stitches and spread them along the length of the circular needle, making sure that the row is not twisted. Mark the first stitch with a contrast thread or stitch marker to keep track of how many rows you have worked.

To create a flat piece of knitting using knit and purl rows, turn the work at the end of every row.

If the nylon cord between the needles is prone to curling, place the needles in hot water for a few minutes and ease out the curl by running the nylon between your fingers.

Double-pointed needles

Double-pointed needles usually are available in sets of four. Divide the stitches evenly between three of the needles and, once the cast-on row has been made, use the fourth needle to knit. Once all the stitches from one needle have been knitted onto the fourth, use the free needle to work the stitches along from the next needle. Keep the tension of the stitches constant when transferring from one needle to another; always draw the yarn up firmly when knitting the first stitch at the change-over point to avoid a ladder or loopy stitch.

As with circular needles, ensure the cast-on row is not twisted before you start knitting and use a stitch marker to identify the first stitch.

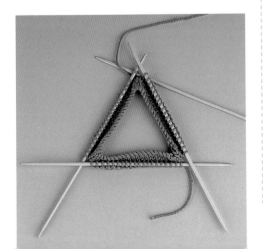

LENGTHS OF CIRCULAR NEEDLES AVAILABLE AND MINIMUM NUMBER OF STITCHES REQUIRED

Inch	4 in (10 cm)	16 in (40 cm)	20 in (50 cm)	24 in (60 cm)	28 in (70 cm)	32 in (80 cm)	40 in (100 cm)	48 in (120 cm)
3	12	56	69	81	95	109	136	160
3 ½	14	64	79	93	109	125	156	184
4	16	72	89	105	123	141	176	208
4 ½	18	80	99	117	137	157	196	232
5	20	88	109	129	151	173	216	256
5 ½	22	96	119	141	165	189	236	280
6	24	104	129	153	179	205	255	303
6 ½	26	112	138	164	192	220	275	327
7	28	120	148	176	206	236	294	350
7 ½	30	128	158	188	220	252	314	374
8	32	136	168	200	234	268	334	398
8 ½	34	144	178	212	248	284	353	421
9	36	152	188	224	262	300	373	445

Binding off

Once the knitted piece has reached the required length, it needs to be bound off or left on a holder. Without some kind of finishing, a knitted fabric will unravel. There are many different ways of binding off (see page 47), but all need to be neat, slightly elastic, yet firm.

Basic knit bind-off

This is the most common binding-off technique.

Knit the first two stitches from the left needle onto the right. *With the yarn at the back, insert the left needle through the base of the first stitch on the right needle from left to right.

Pick up the stitch, bring it over the top of the second stitch, and slip it off the right needle.

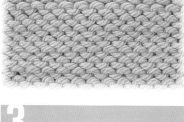

With one stitch remaining on the right needle, knit the next stitch from the left needle and repeat from *.

Basic purl bind-off

This technique creates the same firm edge as the basic knit bind-off, but it is done on a purl row.

Purl the first two stitches from the left needle onto the right. * With the yarn at the back, insert the left needle through the base of the first stitch on the right needle from left to right.

Pick up the stitch, bring it over the top of the second stitch, and slip it off the right needle.

With one stitch remaining on the right needle and with the yarn at the front, purl the next stitch from the left needle and repeat from *.

Abbreviations

The following abbreviations are commonly found in knitting patterns. Abbreviations are used to save space and make written patterns easier to follow. Some pattern writers use slighty different abbreviations, but in most cases there will be a list of abbreviations at some stage of the pattern.

alt	alternate		**ptbl**	purl through back loop
beg	beginning		**p2tog**	purl two together
bo	bind off		**pwise**	purlwise
cm	centimeter		**rem**	remaining
cn	cable needle		**rep**	repeat
co	cast on		**rev St st**	reverse stockinette stitch
cont	continue		**rh**	right hand
dec	decrease		**rs**	right side
dk	double knitting		**sl**	slip
dpn	double-pointed needle		**sk**	skip
foll	following		**skp**	slip 1 stitch, knit 1 stitch, pass slip stitch over
fwd	forward		**ssk**	slip slip knit
G st	garter stitch		**st**	stitch
in.; ins.	inches		**St st**	stockinette stitch
inc	increase		**tbl**	through back loop
incl	including		**tog**	together
k	knit		**ws**	wrong side
kwise	knitwise		**wyb**	with yarn in back
mb	make bobble (*see page 68*)		**wyf**	with yarn in front
mm	millimeter		**ybk**	yarn back
m1	make one stitch		**yfon**	yarn forward and over needle
no	number		**yfrn**	yarn forward and round needle
oz	ounce		**yfwd**	yarn forward
p	purl		**yo**	yarn over
patt	pattern		**yo twice** *or* **yo2**	yarn over needle twice
pfb	purl into the front and the back of the stitch		**yon**	yarn over needle
pnso	pass next stitch over		**yrn**	yarn round needle
psso	pass slip stitch over			

CHAPTER **2**

Finishing
Techniques

Shaping Techniques

To shape a knitted piece, you must learn how to increase and decrease stitches. There are different ways of doing this and most knitters have their own preferences. Decreasing and increasing are also used to create a variety of stitches such as bobbles, cables, and lace patterns.

It is important to know how the stitches will lie with different decreases and increases. For example, when losing stitches around a neck detail, it is preferable that the stitches lie in the direction of the decrease. Stitches on the right side of the neck need to form a slope that points to the right, and stitches on the left side need to create a slope that points to the left.

Decreasing on a purl or wrong side row to create a slope to the right

Working two or more stitches together on the wrong side of the knitted piece creates a slope to the right on the right side. In abbreviated form, this is written as p2tog.

Put the right knitting needle down through the first and second stitches on the left needle.

Decreasing

Decreasing is most commonly done by working two or more stitches together to form one stitch.

Decreasing on a knit or right-side row to create a slope to the right

Knitting two or more stitches together on the right side of the work creates a slope to the right. In abbreviated form, this is written as k2tog.

Put the right knitting needle up through the second and then the first stitches on the left needle.

Knit the two stitches together and slide both from the left needle.

Purl the two stitches together and slide both from the left needle.

The stitches create a slope to the right

The stitches create a slope to the right

Decreasing on a knit or right-side row to create a slope to the left

There are two ways to do this: either work stitches together through the back (in abbreviated form, this is written as k2tog tb1), or slip and transfer stitches (in abbreviated form, this is written as skp, or sl1, k1, psso).

K2TOG TB1 Work as for k2tog, but put the right needle through the back of both stitches on the left needle.

Decrease on knit side to create a slope to the left

SKP Slip the first stitch by placing the right needle through it as if knitting, and slide from the left needle.

Knit the next stitch.

Using the left needle, pass the slipped stitch on the right needle over the top of the knitted stitch. Work to the end of the row.

Alternative method of decreasing on knit side to create a slope to the left

Decreasing on a purl or wrong-side row to create a slope to the left

This is done by working stitches together through the back as on a right side row. In abbreviated form, this is written as p2tog tb1.

Put the right knitting needle through the back of the second, and then the first stitches on the left needle from left to right.

Purl the two stitches together and slide from the left needle.

Decrease on purl side to create a slope to the left

Increasing

There are many ways to increase and most knitters have their own favorite method. Increasing is usually done on the right side of the work. Patterns do not always specify how to increase and may just give the instruction to "make" a number of stitches. In abbreviated form, this is written as m1.

Increasing by knitting into the back of the bar between stitches

This is a neat increase worked between two stitches.

Work to where the extra stitch is needed. Pick up the bar created by the yarn between the stitches by putting the right needle through it from front to back and place it on the left knitting needle.

Eyelet increases

This is the simplest way to make stitches. It creates a small hole, or eyelet, and is especially useful if you require a decorative detail.

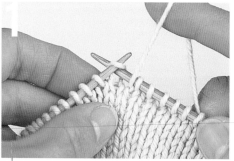

Work to where the extra stitch is needed. Bring the yarn forward between both needles, take it over the right needle and hold at the back. Knit the next stitch. Work in pattern to the end of the row.

On the next row, purl into the loop as if it were a normal stitch and continue in pattern to the end of the row.

Knit into the back of this loop as if it were a stitch and slip it from the left needle.

An eyelet increase worked between two stitches

An increase made by knitting into the back of the bar between stitches

Increasing by knitting into the front and then the back of a stitch

This increase is best worked at either the beginning or end of the knitted piece, as it is not particularly neat. Use it on the edge or one stitch in from the edge, so that it will be lost when the pieces are sewn together.

Work to where the extra stitch is needed. Knit into the front of the next stitch on the left knitting needle without slipping it off.

With the stitch still on the left needle and the yarn at the back, knit into the back of the stitch and slip it from the needle.

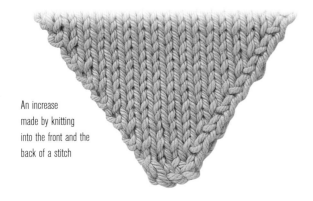

An increase made by knitting into the front and the back of a stitch

Knitting into the stitch one row below

This is another neat increase worked by picking up and knitting into a stitch one row below.

Work to where the extra stitch is needed. Put the right needle through the top right side of the knitted stitch one row below.

Place this stitch on the left needle without twisting and knit it as normal. Continue in pattern to the end of the row.

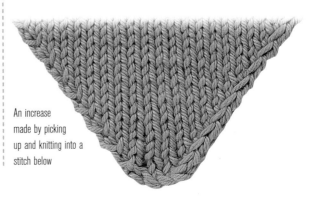

An increase made by picking up and knitting into a stitch below

Fully fashioning

This is the term used to describe visible shaping. The increases and decreases on a fully fashioned garment are worked a few stitches in from the edge and therefore become a feature.

Fully fashioning is often done on garments that have a strong shape or on styles such as a raglan sleeve where the stitches need to lie in a particular direction.

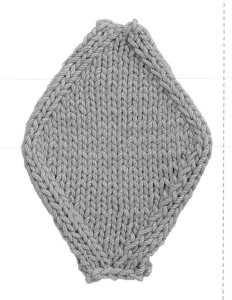

Garment with visible shaping in the waist area

Bias knitting

Increasing stitches on one side of the work and decreasing on the other creates bias knitting. As with fully fashioning, the feature stitches are worked a few stitches in from the edge and form slopes, while the stitches between the shaping remain straight. The angle of the slope depends upon the number of rows between shaping.

Miters and corners

The edge of a blanket or garment may need to fit around a corner in one continuous piece of knitted fabric. A good way of creating a feature to do this is to increase or decrease either side of a central stitch.

An inner corner: This is created by decreasing either side of a central stitch. Work up to the 2 stitches before the central stitch. Decrease by working sl1, k1, psso (skp). K1 (this is the central stitch) decrease by working k2tog, work to end of row. Continue to decrease in this way every alternate row until the angle is achieved.

An outer corner: This is created by increasing either side of a central stitch. Work to the central stitch at the point where the corner is to be placed. Make a stitch (using any of the above increasing methods), k1, m1 and work to end. Repeat on every, or every alternate row, depending on the angle required.

Sewn stitches

Once the knitted piece has been completed, blocked, and steamed, it is ready to be put together. Choosing which technique to use when sewing up a garment could be one of the most crucial decisions you make. Read through the pattern, check that you haven't overlooked any piece, and make a note of any special instructions. (For example, if the garment has a turned-back cuff, you need to reverse the seam for part of the sleeve.)

The most common way of joining knitted pieces is to sew them together. There are many techniques to choose from, but some guidelines remain the same. Ideally you should use the same yarn that you used to knit the piece. However, if the piece was knitted with a fashion yarn such as chenille or mohair, or a particularly chunky or weak yarn, then find a firm, flat thread of the same color.

Attach any pockets, trimmings, or embroidery before you put all the pieces together and sew in any ends.

In most cases there is an established sequence for putting the pieces together. First, join one or both shoulder seams, depending on the style of neckline. Then add the neckline detail or collar. Finally, join the sleeves to the body, and then join the side and sleeve seams.

Sewing in ends

It is possible to sew ends in on one piece or two. Below, the first picture shows sewing in ends on one piece, and the second shows sewing in ends on two pieces.

Thread the yarn through a sewing needle and work a running stitch along the edge of the knitted piece by sewing through "bars" created by the knitted stitches. Tighten slightly and overcast the final stitch. Do not cut the yarn too close to the last stitch as it could unravel.

Seams

It is important to get a neat bottom edge when joining seams. To do this, lay both pieces out flat, right sides together. Thread a sewing needle with yarn and bring it through from the back as close to the bottom and side edges as possible. Make a figure eight with the yarn and needle by bringing it out from the right piece, under and through the left piece from back to front and back under the right and through to the front. This gives a neat start to the seam.

On a plain garment that does not include color work it is a good idea to sew ends in once the piece has been put together. This way you can overcast the yarn end around the seam. Tighten slightly and duplicate the final stitch. Do not cut the yarn too close to the last stitch.

Seam stitches: backstitch

A commonly used stitch for sewing knitwear, backstitch produces a strong but nonelastic edge and is suitable for lightweight yarns. Keep the stitches near to the edge of the work, since this stitch can make seams quite bulky. It is worked with the wrong sides facing you, so it can be difficult to pattern match exactly.

Pin the pieces right sides together, making sure they are matched as closely as possible.

Take the yarn around the outside edge once more, but this time insert the needle through the work from back to front, one knit stitch along to the left.

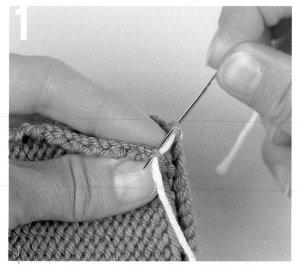

Start by making a securing stitch around the outside edge of the two pieces. Bring the needle through the work from back to front, one knit stitch in from the edge. Take the yarn around the outside edge and back through to the front as close to the original stitch as possible.

Insert the needle from front to back at the point where the first stitch began and bring it back through to the front, another stitch along to the left. Repeat steps 2 and 3, checking that the gauge is not too tight and that the stitches remain matched on the right side.

TIPS

Always sew in good light. If you are using a dark yarn or if the light is poor, thread a contrasting yarn through the stitches to be sewn together to make them easier to see.

Use a new piece of yarn, not one that is already attached to the piece. Make sure the yarn is not too long, since this can cause friction while it is being threaded through the knitted piece, which can cause it to break.

Seam stitches: mattress stitch

Also known as ladder stitch, running stitch, and invisible seam stitch, mattress stitch can be used for any seam and creates a strong, neat join. When worked correctly up a side seam, it should be virtually invisible. Mattress stitch is worked with the right sides facing the stitcher, making it easy to pattern match. The stitches are worked either a whole or half stitch in from the outside edge.

Joining shoulder seams

On the shoulder seam of a stockinette-stitch garment, you can create a really neat and almost invisible seam using a slight variation on mattress stitch.

Place the bound-off shoulder edges next to each other, one above the other with right sides up (to be referred to as top and bottom pieces). Thread a knitter's sewing needle with the knitting yarn. Working from right to left, bring the needle through the center of the first stitch nearest the edge of the bottom piece from back to front.

From the front, put the needle through to the side of the corresponding stitch on the top piece. Bring the needle back through to the front of the work one stitch along to the left.

From the front, put the needle back into the center of the first bottom stitch along, and back up through the center of the next stitch to the left.

Continue to work along the row, making sure that the stitches are the same tension and size as a knitted row.

Joining side seams with mattress stitch

Work on a flat surface with the right sides of the work facing you. Thread a needle with a piece of yarn, and leave the end free of knots.

Join the pieces with the figure-eight technique described on page 35. Having taken the yarn back through the right piece, take the needle across and under the left piece and up through the same hole from which the yarn creating the figure eight comes.

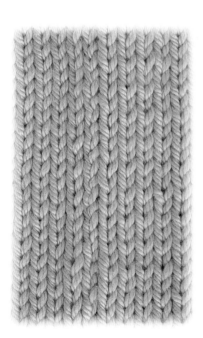

From the front, insert the needle into either the middle or to the side of the next stitch up on the right-hand side. Point the needle up and bring it through to the front two stitches up, so that two bars of yarn lie across the needle.

Take the needle across to the left-hand side and insert it back into the stitch that the last stitch left from. Point the needle up and bring it through to the front two stitches up, again so that two bars of yarn lie across the needle. Work from side to side and pull up the stitches to tighten every couple of inches.

TIP

When an existing ball runs out you will need to join in a new ball. Insert the right needle into the next stitch. Place the new yarn over the working yarn and between the two needles, with the tail end to the left side. Bring the new yarn up from under the existing yarn and knit.

Joining sleeve to body with mattress stitch

A knitted stitch occupies the shape of a rectangle; this is why a knitted gauge does not consist of the same number of stitches as rows. When matching stitches on different planes—for example, vertical to horizontal—you need to take care. With right sides facing you, secure the edges together with a safety pin. Follow the instructions for mattress stitch, working one stitch in on the body and as close to the bound-off edge as possible on the sleeve.

Bring the sewing needle through the center of the edge stitch on the sleeve. From the front, insert the needle in between two stitches on the body and bring through to the front of the work two bars up. Bring the needle through.

From the front, insert the needle back into the stitch on the sleeve that the yarn started from, angle it to the left, and come through the work two bars along.

Continue to work in this way, but take three bars from the body every couple of stitches. This will ensure that the planes ease into each other without stretching.

TIP

When joining a sleeve to the body, mark the center of the sleeve with a pin and match up to the shoulder seam. Thread a piece of yarn through a sewing needle and make a small basting stitch at this point. Do the same at the points where the sleeves meet the side edge of the armhole. This will help you to judge the gauge when sewing the pieces together.

Joining single rib and reverse stockinette stitch

When joining ribs or reverse stockinette stitch, or when using particularly thick or chunky yarns, work the same as for mattress stitch, but work under one bar of yarn at a time instead of two.

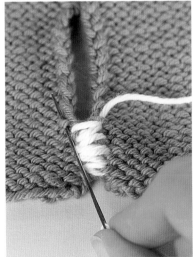

Creating a reverse seam

Reversing seams can look very effective. Work as for mattress stitch on the reverse side of the piece—that is, with wrong sides facing. Alternatively, oversew on the right side, using a sharp needle. When oversewn stitches are worked close together, they create a cordlike seam on the right side.

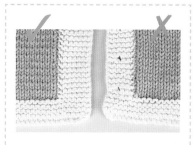

Attaching Bands and Collars

Bands and collars are added to garments to cover and flatten the raw knitted edges. They often determine the fastening method and the use of the piece.

A wide variety of stitches and techniques can be used to join bands and collars. You can use backstitch or mattress stitch, but it is preferable to use a stitch that creates as narrow a seam as possible. Slipstitching and oversewing are both ways of doing this, but they can appear messy if not executed with care.

TIP

When knitting a garment with a sewn-on band, increase one stitch along the inside edge of the band. This makes up for the stitch lost in sewing-up, and prevents the band from pulling in at the bottom.

Slipstitch

Slipstitch can be used to attach any separate pieces, such as patch pockets, front bands, or collars, to the knitted fabric.

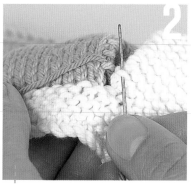

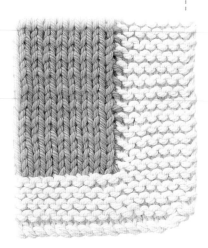

From the front, pick up the bar one stitch in on the piece to be attached. Continue to work in this way, from side to side, pulling up the stitches to achieve an even gauge.

Thread a sharp sewing needle with knitting yarn. Lay the pieces side by side and, stretching the piece that is to be attached very slightly, pin it along the front edge of the garment. Thread the needle through the main knitted piece from the back, picking up the horizontal bar at the center of a stitch.

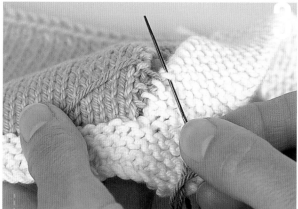

When the top of the piece is level with the top of the garment front, bind off (or leave the stitches on a stitch holder if you're adding a neckband).

Oversewing or overcasting

Oversewing is especially effective on a cuff or area where the seam needs to be as narrow as possible. It is also known as a flat seam.

Place the knitted pieces right sides together, matching the edges exactly. Pin together approximately 1 inch (2.5 cm) in from the edge to give yourself room to hold the work. Work as close to the edge of the work as possible, taking the yarn through both thicknesses of fabric from back to front, over the knitted edge, and along to the left by a few stitches.

Knitted-in bands

It is possible to join a ribbed band that has a slip-stitch selvage directly onto the front edge of a garment as it is knitted. The technique differs depending on whether the band is to be joined on the left- or the right-hand side of the work.

ATTACHING A BAND ALONG THE LEFT HAND SIDE

Cast on and rib one row of the band up to the final stitch, making sure that it is a purl stitch. *With the yarn at the front, insert the right needle purlwise through the next stitch, and also put the needle through the first selvage stitch.

Purl the two stitches together. Turn the work and slip the first stitch knitwise and rib to end. Repeat from *.

ATTACHING A BAND ALONG THE RIGHT HAND SIDE

Cast on and rib one row of the band up to the final stitch, making sure that it is a knit stitch. Insert the right needle knitwise through the stitch on the left needle and through the first selvage stitch on the main piece, and knit together.

Turn the work and slip the first stitch purlwise, with the yarn at the front. Rib to the end and repeat.

Attaching collars

Collars can be knitted onto a garment by picking up stitches or sewn on once the garment is complete. Sew on the collar neatly and evenly, as both sides of the seam can be seen if the neckline is open.

Attaching neckbands

The seam around a neckline follows a curve. When sewing a seam such as this into place, it is important to keep the stitches small and even. The two methods most suitable are backstitch and slipstitch. These stitches are best achieved when the knitted stitches of the completed neckband have not been bound off, but rather left on a contrast piece of yarn that can be removed while sewing.

To join an open collar to a knitted piece, fold it in half, or count the knitted stitches, to find the center. Pin this point to the center of the back neck and join the two pieces with a basting stitch. Repeat to match the front edges.

BACKSTITCHING A NECKBAND

Place the neckband on the neckline, right sides facing upward. Work backstitch from the center and to the center of every stitch on the neckband, removing the contrast yarn from the knitted stitches as you go.

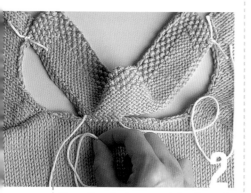

To sew the collar to a garment, thread a needle with enough yarn to sew the whole seam, but do not knot it. Starting at the center back, bring the needle and half the length of yarn through both knitted pieces. (You will use the free end of yarn to sew the other side of the collar.) Slipstitch the collar in place and secure the end of the yarn on the inside edge. Remove the needle, thread it with the free end of yarn, and repeat for the second side.

SLIPSTITCHING A NECKBAND

If working a double neckband—that is, one that is folded—pick up and rib the stitches and work until it is double the required length. Fold to create a double band and slipstitch into place through the center of every stitch, removing the contrast yarn as you go.

Grafting

Grafting is also known as weaving or Kitchener stitch and is used where a seamless join is required. Best used on stockinette stitch, it also can be done on garter and ribs— although this is quite tricky.

Grafting is commonly used to join shoulder seams, or sleeves to body, but it is also a good way of making alterations to existing pieces (see Correcting Mistakes, page 82). As with mattress stitch on a shoulder seam, grafting gives the appearance of a knitted row, but has no seam.

Grafting to join shoulder seams

Leave the pieces on the needles as shown. With knitting yarn, work from left to right, and from the back of the fabric, bring the needle through the first knitted stitch of the lower piece, then through the the first stitch on the upper piece.

From the front, thread the needle back through the center of the first stitch where the yarn leaves, then out of the center of the next stitch along to the left.

Thread the needle back through the center of the top stitch and along to the center of the next. Continue, slipping the stitches from the knitting needle as the row is worked.

Grafting to join sleeve to body

To join differing planes of knitted fabric, such as sleeve to body, a combination of grafting and mattress stitch creates a soft, elastic seam with little bulk.

Lay both pieces flat with the side edge of the garment matched up to the stitches on the sleeve. Work from the first sleeve stitch and around one bar on the body, back to the center and along to the next stitch. To compensate for the differences in stitch to row gauge, take two bars from the body every couple of stitches.

TIPS

It is a good idea to practice any sewing-up techniques before you use them on a garment or finished knitted piece. Use a knitted gauge swatch to do this.

When designing a garment, or working from an existing pattern, check that the knitted pieces will match once the stitches are taken away for sewing up. For example, for a rib to run in pattern across a whole border (i.e. when front and back are joined) you need to add four extra stitches to compensate for the stitches lost when sewing together.

Picking up stitches

Most knitted pieces have an edging or border of some kind to neaten the edge and prevent the fabric from curling. While lace edgings and tassel-type edgings are generally sewn onto the piece, ribs and bands tend to be worked by picking up stitches.

Stitches must be picked up evenly, particularly around necklines since this tends to be the focal point of a garment. Your pattern tells you how many stitches are needed for an even pickup, but remember that if the length or size of the garment has been changed, the number of stitches for the pickup will alter, too (see Tip). If too few stitches are used, the knitted piece will pucker, and if too many are picked up, then the band will flare. Stitches are picked up either through the whole or half of the edge stitch, using a knitting needle or crochet hook two sizes smaller than that used to knit the bulk of the piece.

TIP

Your pattern tells you how many stitches to pick up. However, if the length or shape of the piece has been changed in any way, or if the garment has been designed from scratch, you will have to calculate yourself how many stitches are needed.

To do this, knit a tension gauge in the stitch used for the border or band. Measure the knitted gauge and work out how many stitches there are to either 1 inch or 1 centimeter. Measure the edge of the knitted piece and then multiply this measurement by the number of stitches. For example, if the gauge is 5 stitches to 1 inch (2 stitches to 1 cm) and the edge is 12 inches (30 cm) long, then you will need to pick up 60 stitches.

Marking the edge for picking up stitches

Measure the edge of the knitted piece and place large-ended pins, markers, or short knotted pieces of yarn at even intervals—for example, every 2 inches (5 cm). To calculate how many stitches to pick up between the markers, divide the number of sections into the number of stitches required.

Picking up stitches along a horizontal edge

Around a neckline or on a blanket or throw, you need to pick up along a bound-off edge. This is done using one needle and with the right side of the work facing you.

Hold the needle in your right hand and insert it through the center of the first stitch below the bind-off from front to back.

Wrap a new piece of yarn around the knitting needle from back to front, as if to knit.

Pull the loop through the knitted stitch to the front.

Picking up stitches along a vertical edge

A vertical pickup is done one stitch in from the edge of the knitted piece, using one needle and with the right side of the work facing you. However, because a knitted stitch is not symmetrical and there are more rows than stitches to most knitted gauges, you do not need to pick up on every stitch.

Insert the knitting needle between the first and second stitches at the bottom corner of the knitted piece.

Wrap the yarn around the knitting needle from back to front and pull the loop through the knitted piece.

Picking up stitches along a shaped edge

When picking up stitches around a neckline or any piece of shaped knitting, pick up one stitch in from the edge to eliminate jagged or untidy shaping.

Be very careful when picking up between the knitted piece and any stitches that have been left on stitch holders or have not been cast off (at the center of the neck, for example). Do not pick up into the center of any obvious holes.

If the neckband is a different color than the body of the piece, pick up the stitches in the main color and change yarns for the first row.

Picking up stitches with a crochet hook

This is a good method to use on tough yarns or pieces knitted to a tight gauge. The stitches are picked up with a crochet hook and then transferred to the knitting needle.

Insert the crochet hook through the knitted piece from front to back between the first two stitches, or into the center of the stitch below the bind-off.

Wrap the yarn around the hook from front to back and pull through. Repeat until all stitches have been made.

Once complete, slip the loop onto a knitting needle, making sure that it is not twisted.

Casting on and binding off techniques

Key techniques are shown under basic knitting skills (pages 16–27). This section covers a few more complicated techniques and shows how to eliminate the need to sew pieces together by binding off two pieces of knitting together.

In some cases, an extra strong cast-on or bind-off may be required, such as on children's garments where cuffs and edges may be prone to hard wear. Elaborate casting-on and binding-off techniques can dramatically change the appearance of an otherwise plain garment: a picot edge, for example, can look especially good on the edge of collars and cuffs.

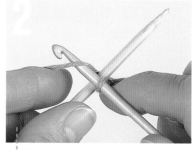

Take the crochet hook over the top of the knitting needle and under the yarn.

Pull the yarn through the slipknot to make a stitch. Take the yarn back behind the knitting needle and repeat from *.

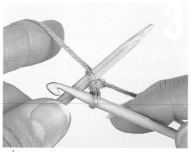

When enough stitches have been made, transfer the last stitch from the crochet needle to the knitting needle.

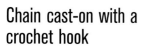

Casting on

The type of cast-on method that you decide to use depends upon the finished outcome. Make a decision as to whether you require an elastic or firm cast-on, fancy or plain. In each case, always make sure that the yarn to be used is free from knots and snags and that you have enough to complete the whole cast-on.

Chain cast-on with a crochet hook

Using a crochet hook to cast on gives a very neat, chainlike appearance. Make sure that the hook is the correct size for the yarn being used.

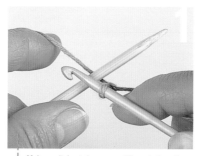

Make a slipknot (see page 17) and place it on the crochet hook. *Hold the knitting needle in your left hand and the crochet hook in your right hand. Take the yarn under the knitting needle and hold it over your left index finger.

Casting on: picot

This cast-on gives a pretty edge and works especially well on collars and cuffs. The picot cast-on can be done with any number of stitches as long as the amount cast on exceeds the number bound off. The example uses a cast-on of six stitches and a bind-off of three.

Using the cable method (see page 18), cast on six stitches. Bind off three stitches.

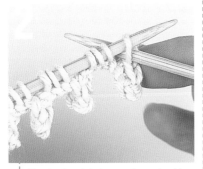

Transfer the stitch that remains on the right needle after the bind-off onto the left. Repeat from*.

Binding off

Once the knitted piece has been completed, the knitting needs to be bound off in some way to prevent it from unraveling. In most cases, the basic bind-off is fine to use, however, you may decide to use a crochet hook for speed or the picot method to create a fancy edge. As with casting on, always make sure that you have enough yarn to complete the bind-off.

Binding off with a crochet hook

This is a very quick and easy way to bind off. Using a crochet hook creates an even and slightly elastic bind-off that is especially good for yarns with little give, such as cotton and silk.

With the right side facing and holding the yarn and the knitted piece in your left hand, insert the crochet hook knitwise through the first stitch on the knitting needle.

*Take the crochet hook over the top of the yarn, catch it over the hook, and bring it through the stitch.

Slip the knitted stitch from the needle and use the crochet hook to bring the second stitch through the center of the first. Repeat from * to end.

Binding off in rib

Rib is mostly used to create an elastic edge around the bottom, cuff, or neckline of a garment. When binding off, it is best to do so in pattern—in other words, to bind off the purl stitches purlwise and the knit stitches knitwise. This keeps the elasticity and prevents the rib from becoming too tight.

Picot bind-off

As with the picot cast-on method, this bind-off produces a feminine picot edge suitable for collars and necklines. The picot bind-off can also be used to create a fancy edge on throws or baby blankets. The number of stitches bound off in one step needs to exceed the number of stitches that are cast on in the next. The example uses a bind-off of six stitches and a cast-on of three.

TIP

Once the knitted piece has been bound off, you will often find that you are left with an oversized or "baggy" last stitch. If the piece is going to be joined to another one (for example, as a side seam), this is not a problem as the stitch will be lost in the sewing-up. However, there are times when the whole bind-off is visible, such as on a blanket or small bag, and so the final stitch needs to be neat.

To do this, bind off every stitch except the last one. Transfer this stitch to the right needle. Using the left needle, pick up the stitch directly under the last. Transfer the slipped stitch back to the left needle and knit off the two stitches together.

* Bind off six stitches using the basic knit method (see page 26). Transfer the stitch on the right needle to the left needle.

Using the cable method (see page 18), cast on three stitches and repeat from *.

Three-needle bind-off

This method is used to join two pieces of work together without having to sew. It is used for holding a pocket, for example, or to join the top edges of a knitted piece, for example shoulder seams. In order for the method to work, the pieces need to have the same number of stitches or, in the case of a pocket, fewer stitches than the main piece.

Transfer the knitted pieces from holders onto knitting needles. The right sides of the work need to be facing each other and the needles need to face in the same direction. (The knitter should be holding both needles in one hand, like chopsticks, with the third needle in the right hand.)

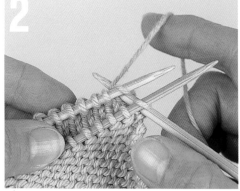

* Hold a third needle, the same size as was used to knit the piece, in the right hand and put it through the front stitch as if to knit, and then the back stitch (i.e., through the first two stitches on both needles held in your left hand simultaneously), and knit off the two stitches together *. Repeat this so that there are two stitches on the right needle.

Garment made using picot bind-off method

Using the back needle in your left hand, bind off the first stitch from the right needle and repeat from * to *.

Turning rows or short-row shaping

These are terms used to describe a process of shaping within the knitted piece without binding off stitches until all the shaping is complete. Turning rows are often used to shape collars, and they are an effective way of shaping shoulders on fitted garments. Working a wrap stitch—where the yarn is wrapped around a slip stitch to avoid a hole when turning, on either a knit or a purl row—creates the shaping. It is wise to plot out on paper the steps that need to be completed before you start work.

Turning on a knit row

Work to where the piece needs to be turned. Slip the next stitch purlwise with the yarn at the back.

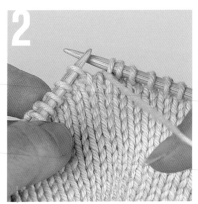

Bring the yarn forward between the two needles.

Slip the stitch back to the left needle and take the yarn to the back through the needles. Turn and work to the end.

THE FINAL ROW

When all the turning rows have been completed, work the wrap stitches to prevent them from showing at the front.

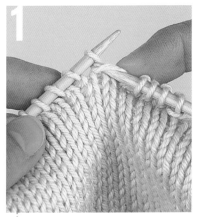

Knit up to the wrap stitch. Put the right needle up through the front of the wrap.

Put the needle up through the stitch above the wrap and knit the two together.

Turning on a purl row

Work to where the piece needs to be turned. Slip the next stitch purlwise with the yarn at the front.

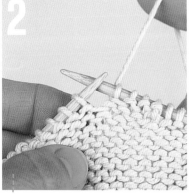

Take the yarn back between the two needles.

Slip the stitch back to the left needle and bring the yarn back through the needles to the front. Turn and work to the end.

Turning rows are often used to shape collars as shown on this garment

THE FINAL ROW

As for a knit row, the wrapped stitches need to be worked to stop them from showing on the front of the piece.

Purl up to the wrap stitch. Using the right needle, pick up the back loop of the wrap.

Place the loop on the left needle and purl this and the first stitch together.

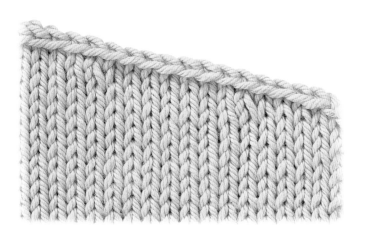

Selvages

The selvage is the very edge stitch or stitches of the knitted fabric. Most written patterns assume that the edge stitch will be worked to pattern—that is, knitted on a knit row and purled on a purl row. However, this is a matter of personal choice. There are ways to work these edge stitches to create neater or decorative edges that prevent the work from curling and make it easier to sew together. Patterns usually allow for a selvage stitch to ensure that ribs and color work match up correctly when sewn together.

Slipstitch selvage

This selvage is popular with some knitters because it creates a neat edge that is ideal for pieces that do not need to be sewn together, such as scarves and blankets. However, because a row of knitting is missed on one stitch, it can make holes and create problems when picking up stitches. To work a slipstitch selvage, simply slip the first stitch on every row to pattern—that is, knitwise on a knit row and purlwise on a purl row.

Garter-stitch selvage

This is best worked on stockinette stitch and can be done on one or two stitches. Knitting the first and last stitch, or stitches, on every row creates the edge.

Decorative selvage

This selvage creates a picot edge on the side of a knitted fabric. At the beginning of the row, simply cast on the number of stitches required using the cable method, then bind them off and work to the end of the row.

Hems

A hem forms an edge on a knitted garment where a rib or knitted selvage, such as garter stitch or moss stitch, would not be suitable. A hem eliminates curling and allows the garment to hang correctly by adding weight to the bottom. Waistbands or cuffs can be created by threading a piece of elastic or ribbon through a knitted hem. A hem is made by working an extra piece of knitting along the bottom edge, which is then folded and sewn or knitted into place. The folded part of the hem should be worked in stockinette or smooth stitch to avoid bulk, and should be worked on a smaller needle than the main body of knitting.

Plain hem

To achieve a neat fold, create a turning ridge once the hem has reached the required depth. The ridge is formed by working one row opposite the rest. In stockinette stitch, this would mean working a row knitwise in place of a purl row.

Picot hem

Eyelets create a decorative turning ridge. Work with an even number of stitches and finish on the wrong-side once the hem is the required depth. Next row: Knit two together, yarn over (k2tog, yo) to end. Turn and continue in stockinette stitch.

Knit-in hem

It is possible to knit the hem before the rest of the garment. Check that the hem is correct before continuing with the pattern, since any mistakes are difficult to rectify without unraveling the knitted piece.

Work as for a plain hem until both pieces, either side of the turning ridge, are the same length, ending with a wrong-side row. Leave the stitches on the needle with yarn attached.

Using a spare piece of the same yarn and a needle of the same size, pick up one loop through the center of every stitch along the cast-on edge (see page 44). Cut the yarn, leaving a small tail.

Turn the work and fold the hem and use a third needle to work across the row, knitting the two pieces together.

Front

Back

Vertical hems or facings

A facing or hem along the front edge of a garment—on a cardigan, for example—can be an attractive design feature. A hem neatens the edge and allows the garment to hang well. It also prevents the fastenings from stretching.

Slipstitch turning ridge

To create a slipstitch turning ridge on a stockinette facing, work to the stitch where the piece is to fold and slip it purlwise on the right side and purl it on the wrong side.

Garter-stitch turning ridge

To create a garter-stitch turning ridge on a stockinette facing, knit the appropriate stitch at the point where the piece is to fold on every row. The vertical row of garter stitch makes the turning ridge (see below, left).

Open   Folded

Open

Folded

Picked-up hem

You can create a vertical facing by picking up stitches along the edge and working them in the same way as for a horizontal hem. To do this, pick up the number of stitches required along the front edge (see page 45). Work until the hem is the correct depth, make the turning ridge, and complete to match the first side of the hem. Then bind off and sew into place.

Open   Folded

Mitered facing

If a piece has a horizontal hem and a vertical facing, you will need to create a mitered corner so that the pieces do not overlap when they are folded into place.

On the hem, cast on fewer stitches than are needed for the turning ridge of the hem and increase to the number needed by increasing every alternate row along the mitre edge. To calculate how many stitches fewer you will need, count the number of rows in the first part of the hem. Divide this by two and take this amount away from the number of stitches required by the cast-on. Make the turning ridge. On the vertical facing, increase every other row as before, adding one stitch for the front turning ridge.

Open

Folded

How to sew hems and facings into place

Once you have completed the knitted hem or facing, you need to sew it into place. It is very important that the stitching is not visible on the right side of the work and that it does not cause puckering.

Fold and pin the hem into place, making sure that the stitches are straight and line up. Sew in a straight line without pulling the thread too tightly. Whipstitch and herringbone are useful stitches for this.

Whipstitch

Whipstitch is suitable for sewing light- and medium-weight yarns into place. Fold the hem, wrong sides together, making sure that the stitches line up, and pin into place if necessary. Thread a large sewing needle and insert it through the loop created by a stitch on the wrong side, and then through the center of the corresponding stitch on the bind-off edge. Bring the yarn through and repeat.

Herringbone stitch

Use this stitch on bulky yarns or ones liable to stretch. Herringbone stitch can also be used over shirring elastic to hold it in place. It is similar to backstitch in that the thread is worked forward and backward.

Working with the wrong side facing, * insert a threaded needle through the stitch just on the inside edge of the bind-off from right to left. Bring the yarn across a few stitches to the right and put the needle through the loop created by the knitted stitch from right to left. Bring the yarn across a few stitches and repeat from *.

Care essentials

After all the effort and time that you put into knitting a piece, don't ruin it by poor care. A garment knitted in a quality yarn can last for many years if it is cared for properly. Before you make any decision about how to wash, block, or steam an item, always check the ball band for as much information as possible.

Washing

The most common outcome of poor care when washing is a shrunken, matted, and dense piece of knitting, commonly known as felting, which is caused by friction, agitation, and heat—or a combination of these.

Although different yarns require different kinds of care, the same general principles for washing apply to most. Do not use a biological washing powder or one with added "brighteners" as these can break down the yarn fiber. Soap flakes, mild detergent, and specially formulated liquids are best: if in doubt, test it by washing the gauge swatch before you wash the finished item. Make sure the water is cool and that the detergent is completely dissolved. If the detergent needs warm or hot water to disperse thoroughly, let the water cool down before you wash the knitted piece.

Do not wring, twist, or rub the fabric. Wash the garment as quickly as possible (although some pieces can be left to soak for short lengths of time). Make sure the water runs clear after the final rinse.

If you are machine washing, use a delicate or wool cold-water cycle with as little fast-spin action as possible. You can buy net bags to put delicate fabrics in, but a tied pillowcase will do just as well.

Drying and blocking

Knitted pieces need to be dried as quickly as possible to avoid them becoming misshapen or developing an odor. The smell arises from the knitted fabric taking a long time to dry and mildew arising. It is important to remove as much water as possible before laying a piece out to dry. Wrap it in an absorbent towel and quickly spin it in the washing machine. Or, you can wrap the item in a towel and apply pressure. The towel will absorb excess water.

Blocking is the term to describe laying a piece flat to reshape it once it has been washed. Keep in mind the original measurements of the knitted piece before blocking. Reshape the piece and lay it out flat on a dry towel or a raised sweater dryer, protecting the surrounding area with plastic sheeting if need be. Leave it to dry away from direct sunlight and turn it occasionally. Blocking a garment while it is still damp should eliminate the need for you to press it once it is dry.

HAND WASHING	MACHINE WASHING	BLEACHING	PRESSING	DRY CLEANING
Do not wash by hand or machine	86°F 30° Machine washable in warm water at stated temperature	Bleaching not permitted	Do not press	Do not dry clean
Hand washable in warm water at stated temperature	86°F 30° Machine washable in warm water at stated temperature, cool rinse and short spin	CL Bleaching permitted (with chlorine)	Press with a cool iron	Ⓐ May be dry cleaned with all solutions
	104°F 40° Machine washable in warm water at stated temperature, short spin		Press with a warm iron	Ⓟ May be dry cleaned with perchlorethylene or fluorocarbon or petroleum-based solvents
			Press with a hot iron	Ⓕ May be dry cleaned with fluorocarbon or petroleum-based solvents only

Blocking is also used to describe laying out pieces of a garment before sewing them together. If a piece is prone to curling you may need to pin it. Pieces to be joined together should be blocked with the right side facing down and then secured using large-headed pins. If necessary, ease the fabric to achieve the correct measurements.

Steaming and pressing

You may need to steam or press a piece of knitting. Pin out the piece as described for blocking. Place a damp cloth over the fabric and press with the iron. For cabled or textured pieces, hold a steam iron over the top of the cloth and allow the steam to pass through to the knitted fabric.

Never place a hot iron directly on a knitted fabric as it can cause irreparable damage—particularly to synthetic or man-made fibers. Ribs and cables should be handled carefully as they can loose elasticity if pressed or oversteamed.

STORING

Knitted garments need to be stored flat and as loosely as possible. Moths are especially attracted to dirt, oils, and animal proteins so take special care of yarns that contain lanolin and natural oils. When storing garments for long periods of time—for example, over the winter—wrap them in tissue or brown paper and then cover with a clear plastic bag. To discourage moths, place pieces of cedar or mothballs in the bag.

Before you store dry-cleaned garments, hang them out to air for a while to remove chemical odors.

TIP

To make a blocking board, place a thin sheet of batting between a piece of hardboard and some checked or gingham-type fabric, stretch the fabric tightly (making sure you don't pull the checks out of alignment), and fix in place with staples or tape. When blocking, match the edges on the knitted pieces with the check design on the fabric; this will ensure that they are straight.

RECYCLING YARN

Once a fiber has been left knitted for a length of time, ridges will be created where the stitches were formed. When the yarn is unraveled, it will be loopy in appearance and is therefore unsuitable for reknitting in this form.

To make it suitable for reuse, first roll it into balls and then wind it into hanks, securing it with a small piece of yarn knotted around the yarn at both ends. Either wash or steam the hanks, tie a weight—such as one traditionally used with scales, or a small bag of marbles—at the bottom, and hang. Once the hanks are dry, roll the yarn into balls to be ready for use as normal.

Additions

Whether you are working from an existing pattern or designing a garment from scratch, you can add design features, such as pockets, zippers, or shoulder pads, without drastically altering the appearance of the piece. Always decide whether you are going to do this before you start work, since it involves a little forward planning and some simple calculations.

TIP

The lower edge of a patch pocket can be sewn in place using duplicate stitch (see page 98). Make sure that the stitch is worked through the pocket and the main knitted piece.

Pockets

If you are going to add a pocket to a design, you need to think about the overall appearance of the finished piece. The pocket must be in proportion to the rest of the garment and at a level comfortable for the hands to reach and sit in. If you are adding a pocket to an existing pattern, always allow for extra yarn.

The most common pockets are patch, horizontal inset, and vertical or slanted inset.

Patch pocket

This is probably the easiest type of pocket to use on knitwear and is, as the name suggests, a separate knitted square or rectangle that is sewn onto the main piece. The size and shape is a matter of personal choice, but for an adult hand the average size should be at least 5 inches (12.5 cm) square. When attaching a pocket to a garment, make sure that the knitted patch is even, and neatly knitted. Pin the patch onto the garment to check the position, making sure that it is not too close to the bottom edge of the garment and does not cover any welts or bands. If you are using a dark-colored yarn or if the knitted stitches are difficult to differentiate, mark the position of the pocket with a contrast yarn or by weaving a needle through the garment before you sew the pocket in place.

MARKING THE POSITION WITH A CONTRAST YARN

Block and press the patch pocket and pin it to the main piece. Using a basting or running stitch and yarn in a contrasting color, mark the outline. Make sure that the sewn stitches run in line with the knitted stitches. Overcast the pocket in place (see page 41).

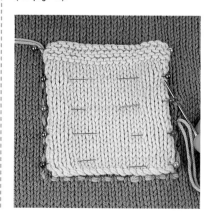

MARKING THE POSITION WITH A NEEDLE

Block and press the patch pocket. Mark its position on the garment using pins without pinning the patch in place.

Thread a knitting needle vertically through one half of the knitted stitches to either side of the pocket, and a third needle horizontally through one half of the knitted stitches below the pocket.

Pin the pocket in place. Sew in place using the overcast method, threading the sewing needle through one side of the edge stitches on the pocket and the corresponding stitches held on the knitting needle.

Pocket flaps

Pocket flaps can be picked up or sewn into place. A flap should be the same width as the pocket and should be placed slightly above the top of the pocket. A mock pocket can be made by attaching a flap only, to create the appearance of a pocket.

RECTANGULAR POCKET FLAP

Pocket flaps need to have some kind of a border to prevent them from curling. Garter stitch and moss stitch work well.

TRIANGULAR POCKET FLAP

A triangular flap can be made either by working from the cast-on and decreasing down, or by starting with a small number of stitches and increasing. Triangular flaps work well with a button detail.

CABLE AND LACE POCKET FLAP

Fancy stitches, such as cable and lace, can produce a very decorative pocket flap.

Inset pocket

An inset pocket is not as obvious as a patch pocket. It is made by knitting and attaching a separate lining, which is not visible from the front of the garment. The three main types of inset pocket are horizontal, vertical, and slanted.

HORIZONTAL INSET POCKET

This is probably the most common type of pocket. It is wise to knit and leave the lining on a stitch holder before you start work on the main piece.

With the right side of the garment facing you, work to where the pocket is to be positioned and bind off the number of stitches required for the pocket top. Work to the end of the row.

On the wrong side, work back to the pocket position. Do not knit into bound-off stitches; work the stitches of the pocket lining (held on stitch holder). At the end of the lining, start to knit into the original stitches and work along the row.

ALTERNATIVE METHOD

Instead of binding off the stitches across the pocket top, slip them onto another stitch holder and work the pocket as before. Once the piece is complete, add a pocket top or border by working across the stitches left on the second stitch holder.

A horizontal inset pocket with a border, made using the alternative method

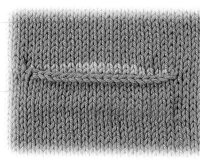

The most common type of pocket—a horizontal inset pocket

VERTICAL INSET POCKET

A vertical inset pocket can be worked on either the left or the right side of the knitted garment.

With the right side facing you, work to the pocket edge and leave the remaining stitches that make up the garment on a stitch holder. Continue to work the front pocket piece to the required length, then place these stitches on a second stitch holder.

With the right side facing you, slip the stitches on the first stitch holder onto a needle facing toward the center of the garment. Rejoin yarn, cast on the number of stitches needed for the pocket lining. Work the lining to the length of the pocket front.

Position the lining behind the front of the pocket and knit the two sections of knitting together (see page 49).

SLANTED INSET POCKET

Work as for a vertical inset pocket, but create a slope on the edge by decreasing stitches.

Zippers

Different weights of zipper are suited to different types of garment and yarn. For example, a jacket knitted in a chunky yarn would need a heavy zipper. The zipper should be the same length as the knitted edge to prevent puckering or stretching, and should be sewn in by hand. Work a garter-stitch selvage for a neat edge. When positioning the zipper, make sure the edge of the selvage overlaps it to prevent the teeth from showing.

With the right side of the garment facing you and the zipper closed, pin the zipper in place so that the edges of the knitted fabric cover the teeth.

Using a contrast thread, baste the zipper in place (see page 79) and remove the pins.

With the wrong side facing and using a thread the same color as the yarn, whipstitch the zipper in place (see page 55). Using a contrast thread, baste the zipper (see page 79) and remove the pins.

Turn to the right side and backstitch the zipper into place, using the knitting yarn if it is fine enough, otherwise a sewing yarn of the same color.

Shoulder pads

Knitted shoulder pads can add shape to knitwear and look particularly nice inside jacket-style cardigans and coats.

The yarn weight and knitting needle determine the size of the pad, but the basic pattern remains the same. The pad is shaped by increasing on the outside edges and decreasing at the center.

TIP

Sewing a shoulder pad in place can create a visible ridge on the shoulder seam and could be difficult to unpick. Instead, attach it inside the garment using a small piece of Velcro.

To make a bulky shoulder pad, work two pads following the pattern above, sew them together, and stuff the center with a small amount of batting.

How to make a shoulder pad

Cast on 3 stitches and, using garter stitch throughout, increase to 21 stitches by making a stitch at each end of the next and every alternate row.

Decrease row: Mark the center stitch and, with right side facing, work to the stitch before the marker. Slip the next stitch, knit 2 together, then pass the slipped stitch over. Work to the end of the row, so you now have 19 stitches.

Work another 6 rows, increasing one stitch on the outside edges of alternate rows to give 25 stitches.

Repeat the decrease row to give 23 stitches.

Increase as before on alternate rows, to give 29 stitches.

Repeat the decrease row to give 27 stitches.

Bind-off row: Make a stitch at the beginning of the row, then bind off the whole row.

Buttons and buttonholes

The overall appearance of a garment is largely determined by the way it closes, so you should think about how you're going to fasten a garment early on in the design process. Buttons tend to be the most popular of all fastenings, since they are generally lightweight, easy to attach, and do not stretch the knitted fabric. If you are working from an existing knitting pattern, you can select the buttons once the piece is finished. However, if you have specific buttons that you wish to use, then it is wise to think about the size and shape of the buttonhole in advance.

Make sure that the button is not too heavy or bulky and will not stretch the garment or catch on the yarn. It is a good idea to buy an extra button and sew it to the inside of the side seam in case it is needed for repairs.

How to choose buttons and buttonholes

Buttons are made in a variety of materials from wood, bone, and mother of pearl to gold, silver, and copper. Mass-produced buttons are made from plastic and glass. Most buttons come with either 2 or 4 holes through the center, or with a shank made from a metal loop.

"Natural" buttons such as horn or wood work well on traditionally styled knitwear such as Aran. Fancy buttons such as gold or diamante are more suited to cotton and silk. The other thing to consider when choosing a button is the size of the buttonhole. This depends primarily on the type of yarn used and the style of garment. A garment knitted in chunky yarn requires a large button—preferably one with a shank—and therefore needs a large buttonhole. A buttonhole for a flat sewn-through button is smaller than the one for a raised button.

How to sew a button in place

If a button is not attached to the knitted piece correctly, it can pull and stretch the fabric. If the garment has been worked in a lightweight yarn such as a 4-ply, then you can use the same yarn to attach a button. For thicker, chunkier knits, use a sewing thread of the same color.

Use a long length of yarn, knotted at one end, and a sharp sewing needle. Sew the button in place either through the holes or the shank, depending on the type of button selected.

Once the button is secure, wrap the yarn around the sewn stitches between the button and the garment at least three times. Secure the yarn on the reverse of the fabric.

How to make buttons

In some cases, you may not be able to find a button that is suitable for your garment. Making the button, as well as the knitted piece, will create a truly original and personal project.

Dorset buttons

Dorset buttons can be made in almost endless permutations of color or just one color. Dorset buttons are especially effective on cushions and garments that require larger buttons since small ones can be tricky to make.

Using a long length of yarn, sew around the edge of a small curtain ring using buttonhole or blanket stitch (see page 80). Holding the tail end of the yarn close to the ring, sew around both the ring and the tail until it has disappeared. Secure once the ring is full and turn the hem edge of the blanket stitch to the inside of the ring.

Using a second yarn, sew around the ring to create a web effect. Using two or three stitches, oversew the center of the spokes and secure the yarn.

Using a third yarn, thread the needle through from the back to the front of the button, close to the center of the web, between two spokes. Fill in the ring's center by working backstitch around the spokes. Fasten off the yarn.

Knitted bobble

A knitted bobble, or round ball, can be used as a substitute for a button, provided it is made in a fairly substantial yarn. Bobbles look effective on Aran or cable designs and can be used with a loop fastening. It is wise to use a knitting needle smaller than the one used to knit the piece.

Cast on 3 stitches. Knit 1 row.
Next row: Increase into first stitch, k1, then increase into the last stitch. Turn and knit to end. Continue to increase in this way on every alternate row to the required number of stitches. (The more stitches, the larger the bobble.) Work one row. Decrease the stitches by knitting 2tog tbl. Knit to last 2 stitches, k2tog. Work 1 row. Continue to decrease in this way on every alternate row until 3 stitches are left. Bind off. Stitch running stitch around the edge and pull up the thread to form a bobble. Secure ends of yarn and sew bobble in place.

Embroidered buttons

You can buy button kits that consist of a two-part button: one side acts as the front, and the other side has a slot that holds the shank in place. Fabric is placed over the front of the button and then clipped into place with the second piece.

Spacing buttonholes

Buttons should be spaced evenly along the button band. It is better to have too many than too few, since this prevents gaping.

Sew down the button band first, then place markers on the band. The bottom and top markers should be placed ½ inch (1.5 cm) from the edge, and the rest spread evenly between. Count the number of rows between the markers and knit the holes to correspond.

Horizontal holes should be placed directly opposite the marker and centered on horizontal bands. Remember to allow two rows for a horizontal two-row buttonhole. Vertical holes should begin slightly below the marker and end slightly above it. Try to allow two or more stitches either side of a vertical hole to reduce the risk of stretching.

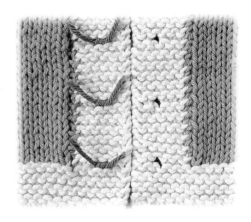

Eyelet button hole

The simplest and smallest buttonhole is the eyelet; it can be worked over 1 or 2 stitches.

YARN OVER 1 STITCH ON A KNIT ROW With the right side facing you, work to the position of the buttonhole. Make a stitch by making a yarn over.

Holding the yarn at the back, knit the next 2 stitches together. Work to the end of the row.

YARN OVER 1 STITCH ON A PURL ROW With the wrong side facing you, work to the position of the buttonhole. Make a stitch by making a yarn over.

Holding the yarn at the front, work the piece, purl the next 2 stitches together, and work to the end of the row. In both instances work the next row in appropriate stitch incorporating the new stitch into the pattern.

TO MAKE AN EYELET OVER 2 STITCHES

To make a larger eyelet buttonhole, wrap the yarn around the needle twice. There are two ways of doing this:

VERSION 1

Work to the position of the buttonhole. Knit the next two stitches together; wrap the yarn around the needle twice.

Slip the next stitch, knit the following stitch, then using the left needle pass the slipped stitch over the top of the knitted stitch on the left needle. Work to the end of the row. On the second row, purl into the first yarn over, then purl into the back of the second.

VERSION 2

Work to the position of the buttonhole. Wrap the yarn around the needle twice.

Knit the next two stitches together through the back of the loop. Work to end of row. On the second row, purl into the first yarn over, and drop the second. A large buttonhole for bulky yarn.

Horizontal buttonhole over one row

This is a strong, quick buttonhole worked over one row.

Work to the position of the buttonhole. Bring the yarn forward between the needles and slip the next stitch purlwise.

Take the yarn back, * slip the next stitch purlwise. Use the left needle to pass the wrapped stitch over the top of the second stitch on the right needle. Repeat from * until the required number of stitches have been bound off. Slip the final stitch onto the left needle.

Turn the work and, using the cable method, cast on the required number of stitches, plus one extra, bringing the yarn to the front between the last two stitches, as for the two-row buttonhole.

Turn so that the right side is facing you, with yarn to the back, and slip the next stitch from the left needle. Using the left needle, pass the extra stitch on the right needle over the top of the slipped stitch. Continue to the end.

Horizontal buttonhole over two rows

This buttonhole is made by binding off the number of stitches required by the buttonhole on one row and then casting them on the following row.

On the first row, work to the position of the buttonhole, bind off the required number of stitches by passing one stitch over the top of the next, and work to the end.

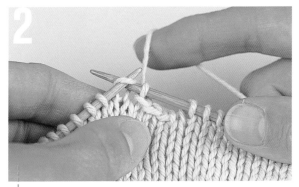

On the next row, work to the bound-off stitches, turn, and, using the cable method, cast on one less stitch than was bound off.

Bring the yarn forward between the last two stitches before placing the last cast-on stitch on the left needle. Turn the work again and complete the row.

TIP

When working buttonholes using a silk or rayon thread, mix in a strand of sewing cotton in the same color to help reinforce the hole. If extra reinforcement is needed, sew around the hole using a buttonhole stitch (see page 67).

Knitted loop

This is a very quick way of creating a loop to fasten a button. It is made by casting on the required number of stitches and immediately binding them off on the next row.

Sewn loop

This is worked in much the same way as a Dorset button, by sewing around a small loop of yarn. Sewn loops are very effective when used with buttons that have a shank. This method can also be used over a crochet loop.

Mark the position of the buttonhole using pins or a knotted yarn. Thread a large needle with the yarn and make a loop by bringing the yarn through the knitted piece from back to front and in by one stitch at the first marker.

Take the yarn back through the work at the second marker and then through by the first marker for a second time. Work buttonhole or blanket stitch around the loop until it is complete (see page 80).

Finishing buttonholes

In some cases, you may need to reinforce the buttonhole using a sewing method.

Blanket stitch

Fine-ply knitting yarn can be used for sewing around a hole, but you may need to split a thicker yarn.

Work from right to left, with the needle pointing to the center of the hole. Space stitches evenly and not too close together so that the hole does not stretch (see page 80).

Overcasting or oversewing

This method works well on smaller eyelet buttonholes.

Simply overcast neatly around the buttonhole using either the whole or a split piece of the knitting yarn (see page 41).

Embellishments

The word "embellish" means to beautify, adorn, or add detail. Simple embellishments, such as a fringe on the bottom edge of a cardigan, can look stunning and are incredibly easy to achieve. More complex additions, such as knitted lace and embroidery, take time but enable you to create a completely original and special piece. All the embellishments in this chapter can be added to a knitted item without any effect on its shape and, with the exception of beads and sequins, are added once the piece is complete.

Bobbles

A bobble, or round ball, is created by working on a small number of stitches within the knitted piece to make a section that stands in relief. Traditionally, bobbles are worked alongside cable work and Aran patterns; however, they are equally effective when used on plain knitting to make a fancy edge or relief pattern—in clusters to create the appearance of a bunch of grapes, for example. Bobbles can also be knitted separately and sewn on once the main piece is completed.

To make a bobble within a knitted piece

A bobble can be worked over as many stitches as you choose. The more stitches and rows you work, the bigger the bobble.

Work to where the bobble is to be placed. Increase into the next stitch by knitting into the front and then the back of the stitch until you have the required number of stitches. 4 or 5 stitches will be sufficient.

Work on these stitches only in either stockinette or garter stitch, for 5 or 7 rows, ending with the wrong side facing.

Slip all the stitches used to make the bobble over the top of the first. Work to the end of the row as required.

To make a separate bobble

Knitting bobbles separately and sewing them on once the knitted piece is completed is a great way of adding embellishment to a finished piece. Work a separate bobble on a slightly finer needle than that used for knitting. The firmer the bobble is, the less likely it is to squash. Always leave a long end of yarn attached to the bobble to sew it in place.

TIP

With a little imagination, you can use bobbles to create three-dimensional "pictures" of fruit, vegetables, or flowers! Pin the bobbles in place first, and then sew them onto the knitted piece when you are happy with their positioning.

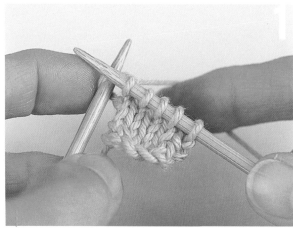

Cast on the required number of stitches (the more stitches, the larger the bobble). Five or six are usually sufficient. Work an uneven number of rows in either stockinette or garter stitch until the piece is the required length, ending with the wrong side facing.

Slip all the stitches used to make the bobble over the top of the first. Cut the knitting yarn approximately 8 inches (20 cm) from the needles and pull it through the remaining knitted stitch.

Thread a knitter's sewing needle with the end of yarn still attached to the bobble and sew a running stitch around the outside edge of the bobble. Pull up tightly and secure.

Tassels

Tassels can look very effective sewn to the corners of cushions or placed on the end of knitted cords. Simple tassels are very easy to make and can add a unique finishing touch to the knitted piece. Tassels can use up a lot of yarn, so make sure that you have plenty and make them once the knitted piece is complete.

1 Wrap the yarn around a piece of cardboard that is the length of the tassel required.

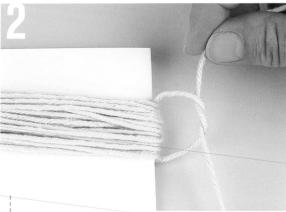

2 Thread a second piece of yarn through the top end of the tassel between the yarn and the cardboard and tie to secure, leaving a long end of yarn to tie around the tassel.

3 Cut along the yarn at the bottom edge and remove the cardboard. Thread the long end of yarn through a knitter's sewing needle and down through the center of the tassel from the top.

4 Wrap the yarn around the tassel as many times as required. Thread the needle through to the top of the tassel and trim.

Pom-poms

Pom-pom making is a very popular pastime for small children and is a fantastic way to introduce them to yarns and the concept of knitting. Pom-poms can look lovely hanging from shelves or a Christmas tree and are particularly effective on cushions and winter hats. You can buy a ready-made pom-pom maker, but circles of cardboard work just as well. Cut two circles bigger than the required diameter of the pom-pom, with a smaller hole at the center.

Knitted cushion embellished with pom-poms

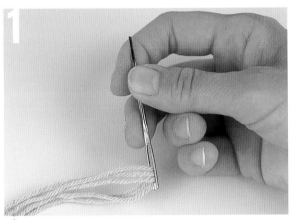

1. Thread a large sewing needle or bodkin with as many ends of yarn as it will take. The yarn ends should be approximately 3 feet (1m) long.

2. Hold the two discs of the pom-pom maker together and thread the needle through the center, around the outside and back through the center from the front, holding the tail end of yarn in place with your thumb if need be. Continue to do this until the central hole is full.

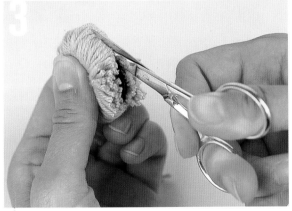

3. Using a sharp pair of scissors, cut around the pom-pom, between the two discs.

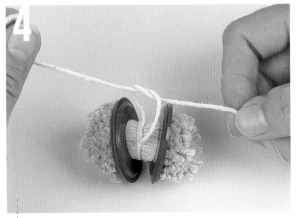

4. Tie a piece of yarn or sewing cotton around the center of the pom-pom as tightly as possible and remove the discs. Trim the pom-pom to form a ball.

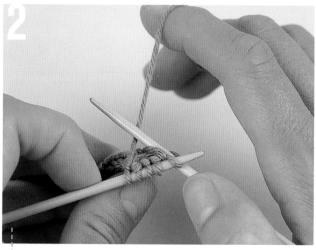

Knitted cord or i-cord

A knitted cord can be used in place of a button as a tie or as a border on a cushion or blanket. Knitted cords are very time-consuming to make, and require the use of double-pointed needles.

Cord using knit stitches

Cast on the required number of stitches. (Four or five are usually sufficient.) Knit one row. * Without turning the needles, move the stitches down the left needle, from left to right, and up to the point.

Bring the yarn across the back of the work from left to right and pull tightly. Knit the next row as before and repeat from * until the cord is the required length. Bind off.

TIPS

Knitted cords can be used to create the effect of a cable when worked in long lengths and sewn onto the knitted piece.

Cords can be twisted together to make an edging (for a cushion, for example). This can look particularly effective in two colors.

Spool or French knitting

This is another great way of getting children interested in yarns and knitting. Spool knitting creates a circular tube similar to that created by knitting a cord on double-pointed needles. You can buy special knitting spools to create the cord; alternatively, use an empty sewing thread spool with four small nails in the top.

Thread the yarn through the center of the spool, with the tail end emerging from the bottom. Wrap the yarn around each peg or nail clockwise, pulling tightly.

Working each stitch separately, wrap the yarn around the back of the next peg and transfer the existing wrapped stitch over the top with a blunt needle or small crochet hook. As you continue, the cord begins to emerge below from the center of the spool.

When the cord is the required length, bind off by moving the last stitch worked along to the next peg. Transfer the stitch over the top of it and repeat until one stitch remains. Cut the yarn and pull through the final stitch.

Twisted cord

Twisted cords can be made with any number of threads and look very effective when different color combinations of yarn are used.

Tie as many yarns together as required using a slip knot and secure by slipping the loop over a pin or sticking it down with masking tape. Twist the yarn in one direction until it is tight.

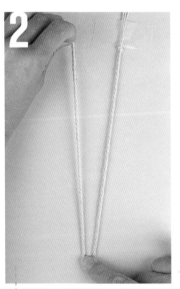

Hold the end firmly in your left hand and pinch the middle of the yarn with the thumb and forefinger of your right hand. Take the end in your left hand up to the secured end and let go of the piece held down by your right hand.

The yarn will twist itself into a cord. Tie the free ends together and even out any bumps using your fingers.

Knitted flowers

Crochet flowers have traditionally been used to adorn garments and blankets, but knitted ones can look just as effective, especially when used on a very plain piece.

Flowers are knitted separately and then sewn onto a background, either singly or in groups to create the effect of a posy. Think carefully about the yarns used to make the flowers: Fancy yarns, such as chenille and ribbon, work extremely well.

Basic petal

This type of petal is perfect for making flowers with overlapping petals. For a larger petal, cast on more stitches (an uneven number) and work more rows.

Cast on 3 stitches. Working in stockinette stitch, increase 1 stitch at each end on every right side row to 9 stitches. Work 6 rows straight. Start to decrease each side of the petal by working as follows: sl1, k1, psso, k to last 2 stitches, k2tog. Continue to decrease in this way on every alternate row to 3 stitches: sl1, k1, psso, and fasten off.

Basic knitted flower

This flower is knitted in one piece and does not need to be sewn together once completed.

Cast on a multiple of 11 plus 2 stitches. (The more multiples you have, the more petals the flower will have.) Purl one row. Next row: k2, * k1, slip this stitch back onto the left needle. Pass the next 8 stitches over the top of this stitch and off the needle. Take the yarn over the needle twice (yo twice), knit the first stitch again, then k2. Repeat from * to end. Next row: p1, * p2tog, purl into the front of the first yo, then into the back of the second. p1. Repeat from * to last stitch, p1. Next row: k2 tog to end. Purl 1 row. Cut yarn and, using a knitter's sewing needle, thread it through the remaining stitch loops and pull up to tighten. Fasten off.

TIP

Study flowers if you have the opportunity; many complex flower shapes can be made using a combination of the above patterns. For example, use the basic knitted flower pattern to create the center, and then attach petal shapes around the outside edge. Knit a larger basic petal shape in a shade of green or brown to make a leaf.

Fringes

A fringe can add a wonderful finishing touch to the edges of a garment or knitted shawl. Fringing looks lovely when added to the edge of a collar, and can be embellished further by adding beads.

Knitted fringe

This fringe is sewn on once the knitted piece is completed and is worked in garter stitch.

Cast on the number of stitches that, when knitted, make approximately one-fifth the depth of the required fringe. Work in garter stitch until the band is the required length. Bind off the first 4 or 5 stitches.

Adding a fringe using a crochet hook

This is a very simple fringe to make.

Cut lengths of yarn to double the length of the required fringe, plus a little more to allow for the knot, and fold in half.

Unravel the remaining stitches to create the fringe. This may be left as loops or trimmed.

Place the crochet hook under the tail end of the fringing and pull through the loop. As you pull the knot will tighten.

Knotted fringe

A knotted fringe is worked in the same way as a crochet-hook fringe and is subsequently knotted. Allow extra yarn for the knots. Divide every section of fringe in half and knot each half of one together with the half of the next fringe in line.

Beaded fringe

A beaded fringe adds weight to the bottom edge of a piece and creates a sophisticated, "dressy" effect.

Use either the crochet hook or knitted method. Thread a small needle with sewing thread and pass the bead down onto the yarn (see page 76). Knot the end of the yarn and add with a crochet hook.

Beading

Knitting with beads can be done in three ways. The first method, known as "bead knitting," or sometimes "purse knitting," dates back to the 18th and 19th centuries and is worked by placing the bead between two stitches. The second method, "beaded knitting," is worked by wrapping the yarn around a slipped stitch. The third method is worked so that the bead sits within the knitted stitch.

For all three methods the beads are threaded onto the yarn before casting on. You may need to thread the beads onto the yarn in sections: Too many pre-strung beads can make knitting difficult and affect the gauge.

Make a small sample to establish how the beads affect the gauge, whether they will snag or fray the work, and whether they are washable.

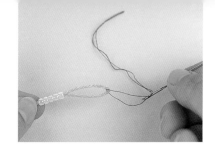

Threading beads

In most cases it is not possible to thread the knitting yarn directly through the bead. To do this, thread the needle using both ends of a piece of sewing thread. Place the yarn through the loop of thread, then pass the beads over the eye of the needle and onto both threads.

Placing a bead between two stitches

This technique was traditionally used for purses. The thicker yarns of today tend to stretch the knitting and the beads may push through to the reverse. However, used in the right way it is quick and easy.

KNIT SIDE

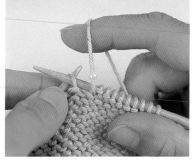

PURL SIDE

Thread the beads onto the yarn and cast on. To place a bead on stockinette or garter stitch, slide the bead up the yarn, and position as close to the knitting as possible. Work the next stitch in pattern.

TIPS

Intricate multi-colored beaded patterns can be created using a graph. Once you've chosen a beading technique, plot out the bead formation on graph paper. Thread the beads onto the yarn in reverse order, reading the graph from top to bottom and from left to right on every beaded row.

When designing with beads, try not to work them too close to the edge of the knitted piece, and bear in mind that stitches will be lost when you sew the item together.

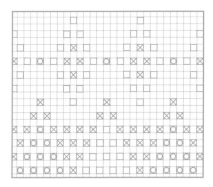

Key: ⊠ Gold bead
⊙ Blue bead
☐ Gray bead

Placing a bead using a slip stitch

Placing beads with a slip stitch is done using garter stitch or stockinette on the right side of the work. Beads can be placed every alternate stitch and every other row. The bead falls directly in front of the slipped stitch.

Work to where the bead is required. Slide the bead up the yarn. Bring the yarn forward between the needles with the bead to the front and slip the next stitch purlwise.

Keep the bead as close to the knitting as possible, holding it in front of the slipped stitch with a finger or thumb if necessary, then take the yarn back between the needles leaving the yarn in front. Knit the next stitch firmly.

Placing a bead within a stitch

Using this technique, the beads are placed on the reverse of the work and pushed through to the front. The bead is held within the stitch and lies at a slight angle on one side of it.

On a right-side (knit) row
Work to where the bead is required. Insert the right knitting needle into the stitch knitwise. Slide the bead up the yarn until it meets the work.

Knit the next stitch, pushing the bead through the stitch so that it appears on the right side of the work. Knit the next stitch firmly.

On a wrong-side (purl) row
Insert the right knitting needle into the stitch purlwise and wrap the yarn around it as if to purl. Slide the bead up the yarn until the bead meets the work.

Push the bead through the stitch to the right side and complete the stitch.

Knitting with sequins

Like beading, sequins add a touch of glamor to a knitted piece. A sequin is a small disc with a hole either in the center or near the top edge. Traditionally sequins were made from glass, but today they are more commonly plastic. Most sequins should not be dry cleaned, steamed, or pressed. Knitting with sequins can be a little trickier than with beads and you need to position them carefully, since sequined knitting is difficult to unravel. All the beading techniques can be used for sequins and there are a few tips that help to anchor the sequin securely and make it lie flat.

Adding a sequin using stockinette stitch

This method is worked on the right side of a stockinette fabric. It is a little time-consuming, but is a strong way to attach a sequin.

On a right-side row Work to where the sequin is to be placed. Slide the sequin up the yarn to the work and bring the yarn forward between the needles. Purl the stitch holding the sequin in place with your left thumb if need be.

On a wrong-side row Work to the position of the sequin. Twist the next stitch by slipping it through the back loop and then replacing it on the left needle. Bring up the sequin and purl the twisted stitch, holding the sequin in place with your thumb.

Adding a sequin using purl stitch

This method can be used on either the right or wrong side of stockinette stitch. On a right-side row, a purl stitch is worked to the side of the sequin; on a wrong-side row it is worked to pattern.

Work to where the sequin is to be placed. Bring the sequin up to the top of the yarn. Insert the right needle through the back of the next stitch and knit as normal, pushing the sequin through the center of the stitch with your finger.

TIP

If you are using sequins that have a slight cup shape, thread them onto the yarn, using the same technique as for beading, with the cup side facing the ball of yarn. This will ensure that they are the right way on the knitted piece.

Embroidery

Simple embroidery adds a personal touch and can transform a plain garment or knitted piece into a unique, distinctive piece.

On knitted fabrics, embroidery is best worked on an even, flat stitch such as stockinette, although it can look fantastic when used to enhance lace and cable work. A smooth yarn is more suitable; a yarn with a slub or pile may stick or snag. The embroidery yarn must be of a similar weight and content to the yarn used to knit, and have the same care requirements. It must also be colorfast.

Not all stitches are suitable for use on a knitted fabric. Heavy embroidery can stretch the knitting and make the fabric stiff. In all cases, use a sewing needle with a large eye, and once threaded, do not knot the end of the yarn.

If you are using a complicated embroidery design, it may be a good idea to draw it out on lightweight, nonfusible interfacing. Either pin or sew it onto the knitted piece, using a basting or running stitch, and remove it by tearing or cutting it away once the embroidery is complete.

Basting or running stitch

This is the most basic embroidery stitch. It is very simple to do and can look very effective on a knitted fabric if used in the right way with good yarns.

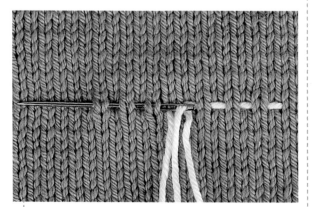

Bring the needle through from the back of the work, then insert it through the piece from front to back a short distance to the left. Bring the needle through from back to front again, a short distance to the left, ensuring that the stitches are of similar size.

Backstitch

This stitch has already been described as a good stitch for joining seams (see page 36). Backstitch is useful for creating outlining and lines.

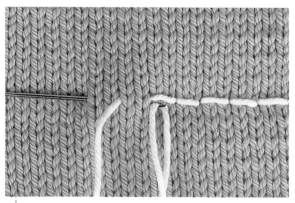

Bring the needle through from the back of the work. From the front and in one motion, take the needle through to the back a short distance along to the right, then draw back through the work to the front the same distance along to the left from the beginning of the stitch. Continue from right to left by inserting the needle through from front to back at the point where the last stitch emerged.

Stem stitch

This creates a line of stitching that can travel in any direction; it is useful for outlining motifs and is worked like backstitch, except that the yarns overlap.

Bring the needle through from the back of the work, then insert it through the piece from front to back a short distance to the right at a slight angle. The distance will depend on how large you wish the stitch to be.

Cross-stitch

Traditionally, cross-stitch is worked on a canvas following a pattern drawn out on a grid. The cross-stitch occupies the space of one or a multiple of squares on the grid.

Cross-stitch works particularly well on a knitted fabric because the knitted stitches are a constant shape and size, making it easy to track and complete complicated patterns.

Work across one or two stitches and rows as required.
Bring the yarn through from the back and make a diagonal stitch to the upper left corner of the "grid." Bring the needle back through to the front at the top right corner, and take the yarn back through the work from back to front and make a diagonal stitch to the bottom left corner.

Chain stitch

As with stem stitch, running stitch, and blanket stitch, chain stitch creates a line and can be worked horizontally, vertically, or in the shape of a curve. Chain stitch is worked in much the same way as blanket stitch in that the loop of the yarn is wrapped around the sewing needle before the stitch is completed.

Bring the needle through from the back. * In one motion, take the yarn through from front to back at the point where the first yarn came through to the front, to create a loop. Bring the needle back through to the front a short distance along to the left and through the center of the loop. Tighten and repeat from *.

Buttonhole or blanket stitch

This stitch can reinforce the edge of a knitted fabric and reduces the likelihood of the fabric edge curling. It is also a good stitch to use to apply appliqué or additional knitted pieces, such as pockets.

Working from left to right, bring the needle through the piece from the back, approximately one row in from the edge of the fabric. From the front, thread the needle through to the back, one stitch to the right, point the needle upward, catch the loop of the yarn around it, and pull through.

Lazy daisy

A quick way of creating the appearance of a knitted flower is to sew a lazy daisy. This stitch is a variation on chain stitch.

Make a chain stitch as described above, but instead of making a running sequence of stitches, sew a small stitch over the top of the chain to hold the loop in place. Repeat this in the formation of a small flower, each chain representing one petal.

Satin stitch

Satin stitch is a very firm embroidery method and is used to completely cover the knitted stitches. It is a good stitch to use to fill spaces outlined by a stem stitch, for example. Be careful not to pull the stitches too tightly, since this will cause puckering.

Make small stitches at a slight angle as close together as possible, by bringing the yarn through from the back and then from front to back the required distance away.

Bullion stitch

This is a variation on a French knot and is worked in much the same way.

Bring the needle through the work from back to front. Thread the needle through from front to back at the point where the yarn emerged, then back to the front, one stitch (or the required length) to the left. Do not bring the needle all the way through. Wrap the yarn around the sewing needle 5 or 6 times. Hold the yarn firmly and pull the needle through. Pull to tighten. Thread the needle through to the back at the point where the very first stitch emerged.

French knot

French knots work really well on knitwear and can add a three-dimensional aspect to embroidery on a flat, knitted fabric. They look especially good as flower centers.

Bring the needle through the work from back to front. Wrap the yarn around the needle once or twice, then take the needle through to the back as close to where the yarn first came through as possible.

Detail of pocket from embroidered jacket (see pages 108–109)

TIPS

It is important that embroidery stitches are worked evenly and neatly. Work on a flat surface to avoid the risk of sewing the knitted pieces together (or to your own clothes) by mistake.

Take your time to plan the design that the embroidery stitches are to form. If need be, sketch your design on drawing or graph paper.

Correcting mistakes

As well as knowing the basic stitches, you must be able recognize and correct mistakes in your work. Check for mistakes at frequent intervals since the method you use to correct a mistake will depend on how quickly you discover it (and, of course, the later you discover a mistake, the more work you will have to do to correct it).

Correcting a twisted stitch

Twisted stitches are made when the yarn has been taken the wrong way around the needle to knit or purl. They are also made when stitches are dropped and put back onto the needle the wrong way around. To correct on a knit row, knit into the back of the twisted stitch. To correct on a purl row, purl through the back of the stitch.

KNIT ROW

PURL ROW

Correcting a stitch dropped on a knit row

Use this method when a stitch has been dropped on a knit row and has not been allowed to unravel more than one row.

Work to where the stitch has been dropped, making sure that the unraveled piece of yarn sits at the back of the fabric.

Insert the right needle through the center of the dropped stitch from front to back and under the unraveled yarn.

Insert the left needle through the center of the dropped stitch on the right needle from back to front and pull the stitch over the unraveled yarn and off the needle.

Transfer the stitch to the left needle and work to the end of the row.

Correcting a stitch dropped on a purl row

Use this method when a stitch has been dropped on a purl row and has not been allowed to unravel more than one row.

Work to where the stitch has been dropped, making sure that the unraveled yarn sits at the front of the fabric.	Insert the right needle through the center of the dropped stitch from back to front and under the unraveled yarn.	Insert the left needle through the dropped stitch on the right needle and lift the stitch over the unraveled yarn and off the needle.	Transfer the stitch onto the left needle and work to the end of the row.

Correcting stitches that have made a ladder on stockinette stitch

If dropped stitches have unraveled for more than one row, they will form a "ladder" or "run" in the knitted piece. The easiest way to correct this is with a crochet hook. Turn the work so that the knit side is facing you.

Make sure that the dropped stitch sits at the front of the work, with the unraveled yarn behind.

Insert the crochet hook through the center of the dropped stitch from the front.

Pick up the first "bar" of unraveled yarn and pull it through the stitch to the front.

Continue to pick up all the bars, and then transfer the stitch to the left needle and work to the end.

Unraveling stitch by stitch

You may need to unravel a knitted piece stitch by stitch to reach and correct a mistake that has been made earlier in the row.

Unraveling a knit row With the yarn at the back and the right side facing, insert the left needle through the center of the stitch below the next stitch on the right needle from front to back and pull the yarn to undo the stitch.

Unraveling a purl row With the yarn at the front and the wrong side facing, insert the left needle through the center of the stitch below the next stitch on the right needle, from back to front, and pull the yarn to undo the stitch.

Correcting color work

If you are using slippery yarn, or are worried about unraveling too much work, it is a good idea to thread a small knitting needle through the row in which the mistake has been made prior to unraveling, to hold the stitches. This is particularly useful if a mistake has been made in color work. It is possible to rework stripes of Fair Isle or areas of intarsia without unraveling the whole knitted piece.

Unraveling rows

It is always safer to unravel while the knitting is still on the needles, but in some cases you may need to unravel more than one row to reach a mistake.

To do this, slip all the stitches from the needle, hold the piece on a flat surface, and pull the yarn gently to unravel the stitches. Keep track of how many rows you have undone, and whether any increasing, decreasing, or design feature has been worked within the area. Place the stitches back on the needle, making sure that they are put on the right way around.

Using a needle smaller than the one used to work the piece, with the right side facing you and working from left to right, pick up the left side of each knitted stitch across the row below and the row above the mistake.

Cut through the center of the piece containing the mistake and unravel.

Correct the mistake by reworking the section and sew in place using the grafting method (see page 43).

Correcting cables

In complicated cable designs, it is common for stitches to have been twisted or cabled in the wrong direction. You can correct them by cutting and retwisting.

Using a small pair of sharp scissors, cut through the top of the center stitch where the mistake has been made on the row that the cable crossed over. Carefully unravel the stitches that make up the cable.

Place the stitches onto knitting needles to prevent them from unraveling.

Before correction

Reposition the stitches and sew them in place using the grafting method (see page 43).

When complete, thread the yarn through to the reverse, and secure.

Corrected

TIP

If a garment needs to be shortened or lengthened, use the same technique as for correcting color work (see page 84). This is also a great technique for mending worn fabrics on areas such as cuffs.

Directory of edgings

Adding a border or edging of some kind can transform a plain garment into something a little more fancy.

Edgings can be simple, textural, scalloped, or lacy and there is no end to stitch alternatives. Edgings can be worked horizontally along the cast-on edge, or vertically as a strip that is sewn in place once it is complete.

Simple edgings are worked over just a few stitches and rows and take very little time to complete. Bobble and lace edgings, which involve increasing and decreasing stitches and a more complex written pattern, can take a little longer, but are a pretty alternative to a plain rib border, for example. More elaborate edgings, such as lace, tend to work better in a crisp, fine yarn such as cotton, since this gives clear stitch definition and is less likely to stretch.

Before you add a border, think carefully about what style would be most suitable for the garment; a simple border works well on a complex piece, while a lace border is more effective on a plain piece.

Simple edgings

It is a good idea to knit samples of edgings and build up a small collection that you can refer to when choosing which edging to put on a fabric. Simple edgings offer a quick and easy way of transforming a piece and don't take long to make.

Eyelet edging

This is a cast-on border, worked over a multiple of 2 stitches plus 1.

Row 1, 2, & 3: Knit.
Row 4: * P2tog, yon; repeat from * to last stitch, p1.
Rows 5, 6, & 7: Knit.
Row 8: Purl.

Small scalloped edging

This is a cast-on border, worked over a multiple of 11 stitches plus 2.

Row 1: Purl.
Row 2: K2, * k1 and slip the stitch back onto the left needle. Lift the next 8 stitches, one at a time, over the stitch and off the needle, yo twice, knit the first stitch again, k2. Repeat from * to end.
Row 3: K1, * p2tog, drop one loop made from the "yo twice" on previous row, in the remaining loop knit into the front and then the back of the stitch twice, k1; repeat from * to last stitch, k1.
Row 4: K1, p1 to end.

Basic picot

This is a cast-on edging that uses any number of stitches, plus 2 extra at the end of the cast-on.

* Cast on 6 stitches using the cable method, then immediately bind off 3; transfer the stitch on the right needle to the left and repeat from * until the final picot has been made; cast on 2.

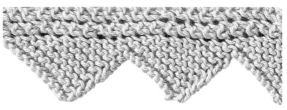

Garter stitch triangle edging

Cast on 7 stitches.

Row 1: K2, yo, k2tog, yo, k to end.
Row 2: Knit.
Rows 3 to 15: Repeat rows 1 and 2 six times more, then repeat row 1.
Row 16: Bind off 8 stitches and k to end.

Repeat the 16-row pattern until the edging is the required length.

Frill edge

Cast on 4 times the number of stitches needed for the main piece of knitting, minus 3 stitches. For a large number of stitches, use a circular needle.

Row 1: K1, * k2, slip the first stitch on the right needle over the second and repeat from * to end.
Row 2: P1, * p2tog, repeat from * to end.

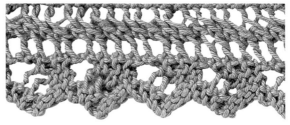

Lacy garter stitch edging

Cast on 10 stitches. (Note that the number of stitches will change from row to row and should only be counted after the 8th row.)

Row 1: K3, (yo, k2tog) twice, yo2, k2tog, k1.
Row 2: K3, p1, k2, (yo, k2tog) twice, k1.
Row 3: K3, (yo, k2tog) twice, k1, yo2, k2tog, k1.
Row 4: K3, p1, k3, (yo, k2tog) twice, k1.
Row 5: K3, (yo, k2tog) twice, k2 yo2, k2tog, k1.
Row 6: K3, p1, k4, (yo, k2tog) twice, k1.
Row 7: K3, (yo, k2tog) twice, k6.
Row 8: Bind off 3 stitches, k4 (not including stitch left on needle after bind-off), (yo, k2tog) twice, k1.

Repeat the 8-row pattern until the edging is the required length.

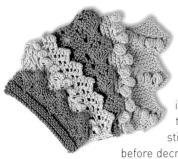

Bobble edgings

A bobble is made by increasing into a stitch and then working on these stitches for only a few rows before decreasing and returning to the main knitted fabric. Bobble edgings look particularly effective on pieces that already have textural stitching, such as cabling, but can be just as appealing as an edge to a plain piece.

Garter stitch with bobble edge

This edging is worked over a multiple of 6 stitches, plus 5. **Note:** To make the bobble (MB), increase into a stitch by knitting into the front and then the back of it until you have 5 stitches, turn, k5, turn, p5, turn, k5, turn, slip the four stitches made by the increase over the top of the original stitch, k1.

Row 1: Knit.
Row 2: K2, * MB, k5; repeat from * to last 2 stitches, k2.

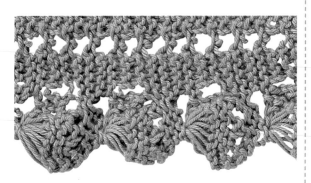

Puff ball cluster edging

Cast on 13 stitches. **Note:** "yo2" means yarn forward twice to make two stitches.

Row 1: K2, k2tog, yo2, k2tog, k7.
Row 2: K9, p1, k3.
Rows 3 & 4: Knit.
Row 5: K2, k2tog, yo2, k2tog, k2, (yo2, k1) 3 times, yo2, k2. (21 sts)
Row 6: K3, (p1, k2) 3 times, p1, k4, p1, k3.
Rows 7 & 8: Knit.
Row 9: K2, k2tog, yo2, k2tog, k15.
Row 10: Knit 12 stitches, wrapping the yarn round the needle twice for each stitch, yo2, k5, p1, k3. (23 sts)
Row 11: K10, (p1, k1) into next stitch, slip the next 12 stitches to the right needle, dropping extra loops as you do so. Pass the stitches back to the left needle and k12tog. (13 sts)
Row 12: Knit.

Repeat the 12-row pattern until the edging is the required length.

Scalloped bobble edge

Cast on a multiple of 10 stitches, plus 1. Make bobble (MB) as for garter stitch with bobble edge.

Row 1: Knit.
Row 2: K5, MB, * k9, MB; repeat from * to last 5 stitches, k5.
Rows 3 & 4: Knit.
Row 5: P1, * yo, p3, p3tog tbl, p3, yo, p1; repeat from * to end.
Row 6: K2, * yo, k2, sl1, k2tog, psso, k2, yo, k3; repeat from * to last 9 sts, yo, k2, sl1, k2tog, psso, k2, yo, k2.
Row 7: P3, * yo, p1, p3tog tbl, p1, yo, p5; repeat from * to last 8 sts, yo, p1, p3tog tbl, p1, yo, p3.
Row 8: K4, * yo, sl1, k2tog, psso, yo, k7; repeat from * to last 7 sts, yo, sl1, k2tog, psso, k4.
Row 9: Purl.
Rows 10 to 13: Knit.

Cast off or continue on main piece of knitting.

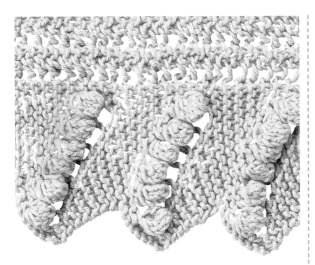

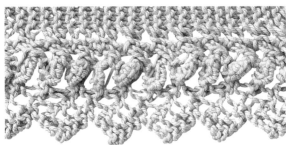

Fern and bobble edging

Cast on 21 stitches.

Row 1: K2, k2tog, yo2, (k2tog) twice, yo2, k2tog, k2, yo2, k2tog, k7. (22 sts)
Row 2: K9, p1, k4, (p1, k3) twice.
Row 3: K2, k2tog, yo2, (k2tog) twice, yo2, k2tog, k1, MB, k2, yo2, k2tog, k6. (23 sts)
Row 4: K8, p1, k6, (p1, k3) twice.
Row 5: K2, k2tog, yo2, (k2tog) twice, yo2, k2tog, k3, MB, k2, yo2, k2tog, k5. (24 sts)
Row 6: K7, p1, k8, (p1, k3) twice.
Row 7: K2, k2tog, yo2, (k2tog) twice, yo2, k2tog, k5, MB, k2, yo2, k2tog, k4. (25 sts)
Row 8: K6, p1, k10, (p1, k3) twice.
Row 9: K2, k2tog, yo2, (k2tog) twice, yo2, k2tog, k7, MB, k2, yo2, k2tog, k3. (26 sts)
Row 10: K5, p1, k12, (p1, k3) twice.
Row 11: K2, k2tog, yo2, (k2tog) twice, yo2, k2tog, k9, MB, k2, yo2, k2tog, k2. (27 sts)
Row 12: K4, p1, k14, (p1, k3) twice.
Row 13: K2, k2tog, yo2, (k2tog) twice, yo2, k2tog, k11, MB, k2, yo2, k2tog, k1. (28 sts)
Row 14: K3, p1, k16, (p1, k3) twice.
Row 15: K2, k2tog, yo2, (k2tog) twice, yo2, k2tog, k18. (28 sts)
Row 16: Bind off 7 sts, knit until there are 13 sts on right needle, (p1, k3) twice. (21 sts)

Repeat the 16-row pattern until the edging is the required length.

Lacy bobble edging

Cast on 12 stitches.

Row 1: K4, yo, sl1, k2tog, psso, yo, k3, yo, k2.
Row 2: K4, increase into the next stitch to make 6 sts, p2, k6.
Row 3: K4, yo, sl1, k1, psso, k2tog, bind off 5 sts, k2, yo, k2.
Row 4: K5, yo, k1, p1, k6.
Row 5: K4, yo, sl1, k2tog, psso, yo, k3, yo, k2tog, yo, k2.
Row 6: K6, increase into the next stitch to make 6 sts, p2, k6.
Row 7: K4, yo, sl1, k1, psso, k2tog, bind off 5 sts, k2, yo, k2tog, yo, k2.
Row 8: Bind off 4 sts, k2, yo, k1, p1, k6.

Repeat the 8-row pattern until the edging is the required length.

The bottom edge of this garment is decorated with a deep garter stitch lace edging

Lace

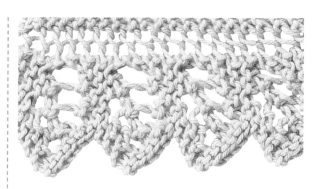

Lace looks wonderful when knitted in fine, crisp yarn and adds a particularly feminine touch to a knitted piece. Lace is created by working stitches together and making stitches by taking the yarn over the needle. Some lace stitches are complex and require a lot of concentration. Try not to leave the piece halfway through a pattern repeat, as lace can be particularly difficult to unpick.

Basic lace edging

Cast on 6 stitches.

Row 1: K1, k2tog, yo, k2, yo2, k1.
Row 2: K1, k into the front and then the back of the yo2 from previous row, k2tog, yo, k3.
Row 3: K1, k2tog, yo, k5.
Row 4: Bind off 2 sts, k2tog, yo, k3.

Repeat the 4-row pattern until the edging is the required length.

Willow lace edging

Cast on 10 stitches. Note: The number of stitches changes from row to row and should only be counted after the 8th row.

Row 1: Sl1, k2, yo, k2tog, * yo2, k2tog; repeat from * once more, k1.
Row 2: K3, (p1, k2) twice, yo, k2tog, k1.
Row 3: Sl1, k2, yo, k2tog, k2, * yo2, k2tog; repeat from * once more, k1.
Row 4: K3, p1, k2, p1, k4, yo, k2tog, k1.
Row 5: Sl1, k2, yo, k2tog, k4, * yo2, k2tog; repeat from * once more, k1.
Row 6: K3, p1, k2, p1, k6, yo, k2tog, k1.
Row 7: Sl1, k2, yo, k2tog, k11.
Row 8: Bind off 6 sts, k6 (this does not include the stitch left on the right needle after bind off) yo, k2tog, k1.

Repeat the 8-row pattern until the edging is the required length.

Feather and fan edging

Cast on multiples of 18 stitches, plus 2.

Row 1: Knit.
Row 2: Purl.
Row 3: K1, * (k2 tog) 3 times, (yo, k1) 6 times, (k2tog) 3 times; repeat from * to last st, k1.
Row 4: Knit.

Repeat the 4-row pattern until the edging is the required length.

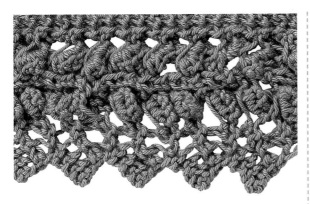

Vintage lace edging

Cast on 13 stitches.

Row 1: K2, yo, sl1, k1, psso, yo, k1, yo, sl1, k2tog, psso, yo, k3, yo, k2. (15 sts)
Row 2: K4, (k1, p1) 3 times into next stitch, p2, k1, p3, k4. (20 sts).
Row 3: K2, yo, sl1, k1, psso, (k1, p1) 3 times into next st, yo, sl1, k1, psso, p1, k2tog, bind off next 5 sts, k to last 2 sts, yo, k2. (19 sts)
Row 4: K5, yo, (k1, p1) twice, bind off next 5 sts, knit to end. (15 sts)
Row 5: K2, yo, sl1, k1, psso, yo, k1, yo, sl1, k2tog, psso, yo, k3, yo, k2tog, yo, k2. (17 sts).
Row 6: K6, (k1, p1) 3 times into next st, p2, k1, p3, k4. (22 sts).
Row 7: K2, yo, sl1, k1, psso, (k1,p1) 3 times into next st, yo, sl1, k1, psso, p1, k2tog, bind off next 5 sts, k to last 4 sts, yo, k2tog, yo, k2. (21 sts).
Row 8: Bind off 4 sts (1st on right needle after bind off), k2, yo, p2, k1, p1,bind off next 5 sts, k to end. (13 sts).

Repeat the 8-row pattern until the edging is the required length.

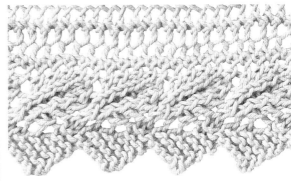

Falling leaf edging

Cast on 17 stitches.

Row 1: K3, yo, p2tog, yo, p2tog, yo, kb1, k2tog, p1, yo, sl1, k1, psso, kb1, yo, k3.
Row 2: K3, p3, k1, p3, k2, yo, p2tog, yo, p2tog, k1.
Rows 3 & 4: Work as rows 1 & 2.
Row 5: K3, yo, p2tog, yo, p2tog, yo, kb1, k2tog, p1, yo, sl1, k1, psso, yo, k4. (18 sts)
Row 6: K4, p2, k1, p4, k2, yo, p2tog, yo, p2tog, k1.
Row 7: K3, yo, p2tog, yo, p2tog, yo, kb1, k1, kb1, yo, sl1, k2tog, psso, yo, k5. (19 sts).
Row 8: K5, p7, k2, yo, p2tog, yo, p2tog, k1.
Row 9: K3, yo, p2tog, yo, p2tog, yo, kb1, k3, kb1, yo, k7. (21sts)
Row 10: Bind off 4 sts (1st on right needle after bind off), k2, p7, k2, yo, p2tog, yo, p2tog, k1. (17 sts)

Repeat the 10-row pattern until the edging is the required length.

Chevron lace frill

Cast on 29 stitches.

Row 1: K5, p16, (yo, k2tog) 3 times, yo, k2. (30sts)
Row 2: K25, turn leaving remaining 5 sts on needle.
Row 3: P17, (yo, k2tog) 3 times, yo, k2. (31 sts)
Row 4: Knit.
Row 5: K18, (yo, k2tog) 3 times, yo, k2. (32 sts)
Row 6: K9, p18.
Row 7: K19, (yo, k2tog) 3 times, yo, k2. (33sts)
Row 8: K9, p19, k5.
Row 9: Knit.
Row 10: Bind off 4 sts, k to end.

Repeat the 10-row pattern until the edging is the required length.

Color work

There are two ways to create different color designs within a knitted piece. In intarsia, areas of color are created using separate ends of yarn. This method produces a single weight of fabric in which many colors can be used on a single row. In Fair Isle knitting, smaller areas of color are created, with subsequent colors carried at the reverse of the work to create a double weight of fabric.

Intarsia

The intarsia method creates separate areas of color within the knitted piece. A separate length of yarn is used for each section of colored knitting, and the yarns are twisted where they meet to create a single piece.

Intarsia is best worked over stockinette stitch, although areas of more textural stitching, such as garter stitch and seed stitch, can also look very effective when used in conjunction with intarsia.

Before you settle down to work, read through the pattern carefully and check how much yarn you need in each color. Intarsia patterns are usually in graph form. Cross off the rows as you work and always check where colors need to be on the row above the one that you are working on, so that you can carry yarns to the correct position if necessary.

To work intarsia effectively you will need to learn a few basic techniques. These are bobbin winding, joining in new colors, and changing from one color to another on both a knit and a purl row.

Bobbins

Bobbins are used when you do not wish to have a whole ball of yarn attached to the knitted piece while working intarsia. Bobbins can be bought ready made and the yarn wrapped around them, or you can make your own. For larger areas of color you may wish to wrap the yarn in small plastic bags, secured with rubber bands.

MAKING A BOBBIN

Wrap the yarn around the thumb and finger of your right hand in the form of a figure-of-eight.

Carefully remove the yarn from your fingers and cut it from the ball. Wind the loose end of yarn around the center of the figure-of-eight and secure it tightly.

When using a bobbin, pull the yarn from the center a little at a time and keep it as close to the work as possible to avoid tangling.

Joining in a new color

You may find that a new color of yarn is needed across a row of stitches, or that an existing bobbin is running out. In these cases you will need to join in a new color.

Changing colors

When working an intarsia design, colored areas of stitching are worked from separate balls. If these areas are not joined together in some way, you will end up with individual pieces of color and no main fabric. Simply cross the yarns to ensure that the knitting stays as one piece.

Insert the right needle into the next stitch. Place the new yarn over the working yarn and between the two needles, with the tail end to the left side.

Changing color on a knit row Work to the point where you need to change color. Insert the right needle into the next stitch knitwise. Take the first color over the top of the second color and drop. Pick up the second color, ensuring that the yarns remain twisted, and continue according to the pattern.

Bring the new yarn up from under the existing yarn and knit, dropping both yarns from the left needle after you have done so.

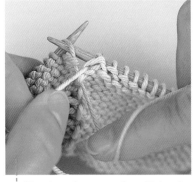

Changing color on a purl row Work to the point where you need to change color. Insert the right needle into the next stitch purlwise. Take the first color over the top of the second color and drop. Pick up the second color, ensuring that the yarns remain twisted, and continue according to the pattern.

TIP

To work out how much yarn you need for an area of color, count the number of stitches it occupies and then wrap an end of yarn around the knitting needle this number of times. This shows you how much yarn the stitches will use, so always allow a little extra for the ends.

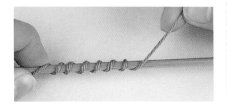

Fair Isle

The term "Fair Isle" is used to describe a method of knitting in which the colors in use are woven across the reverse of the fabric. Traditionally, Fair Isle patterns tended to be small motifs repeated across a row, with only two colors carried at the back of the fabric between stitches, thus creating a double thickness fabric.

Fair Isle is most effective when worked on stockinette stitch, although introducing purl stitches can look effective and adds a little texture to the knitted piece.

Before you start on a garment or other knitted project involving Fair Isle, it is very important that you knit up a gauge sample. Fair Isle tends to create a slightly bulky fabric, and if the yarns are carried across the back too tightly, the piece will start to pucker.

Traditionally, Fair Isle knitting was worked on circular or sets of double-pointed needles, in the round, creating a tubular piece of knitted fabric that was then cut to incorporate sleeves and neckline. Compared with working on two needles, this is a very quick way of working, which eliminates the use of purl rows.

Fair Isle can be worked by holding the yarn in either one or two hands. The basic techniques that you will need to learn are stranding and weaving.

STRANDING

Stranding is where a color that is not being used is carried across the back of the work over the top of the other color without being caught in with the other color. When it is done properly, there should be no tangling of yarns across the row.

It is best to leave not more than three stitches between a change in color, since the yarn can create loops on the reverse of the fabric and get caught or snagged when the piece is in use.

Stranding one-handed

Stranding with one hand involves dropping one yarn after use, then picking up another and carrying it across the back of the work. It is important not to twist the yarns in the changeover between colors.

On a right-side (knit) row Using the first color, knit 3 stitches. Drop the yarn and pick up the second color, carrying it over the dropped yarn, and knit 3 stitches. Drop the second color.

Pick up the first color from underneath the second and bring it across the back of the last 3 knitted stitches. Knit the next 3 stitches, being careful not to pull the yarn too tightly.

On a wrong-side (purl) row Using the first color, purl 3 stitches. Drop the yarn and pick up the second color, carrying it across the last 3 stitches over the top of the dropped color. Purl 3 stitches. Drop the second color.

Pick up the first color from underneath the second, bring across, and purl 3 stitches. Keep the stitches spread out along the right needle to avoid puckering.

Stranding two-handed

Using the stranding technique with two hands is faster than using just one, since the yarns do not need to be dropped between color changes. Hold one color over the forefinger of the left hand (see German or continental method, page 21), and the other according to the style in which you knit in the right hand.

On a right-side (knit) row * Using the first color and the continental method, knit 3 stitches.

Using your right hand, bring the second color across the back of the work, over the top of the first yarn, and knit the next 3 stitches. Repeat from * to end.

On a wrong-side (purl) row Hold the first color over the left thumb on the side facing and the second yarn in your right hand.

Purl 3 stitches in the second color, carrying it over the last 3 stitches. Using the first yarn and the continental method, purl the next 3 stitches.

Correct: When the stranding technique has been worked correctly, the carried yarn sits horizontally over stitches on the reverse of the work.

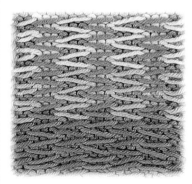

Incorrect: When the stranding of yarns has not been consistent, the yarn sits at a slight angle on the reverse of the work and the yarn ends become tangled.

WEAVING

If a color needs to be carried across the back of the work over more than three stitches, it will need to be caught or woven in. It is best to do this every second or third stitch, since weaving on every stitch can distort the shape of the knitted stitch and weaving too infrequently creates loops. As with stranding, weaving can be done using either the one-handed or two-handed method.

WEAVING ON THE WRONG SIDE
Work to the point where the second color needs to be caught in. Bring the second color up from under the one in use and around the right needle from right to left, anchoring it in place with your left thumb at the front of the work.

Weaving using one hand

As with stranding, weaving with one hand involves picking up and dropping the yarns in use.

WEAVING ON THE RIGHT SIDE
Work to the point where the second color needs to be caught in. Bring the second color up from under the one in use and over the right needle and your left forefinger from right to left.

TIP

When using the one-handed method, you may find it easier to place the carried yarn over both knitting needles instead of just the right one, being careful not to work both yarns into either the knit or the purl stitch.

Using the right needle, purl the next stitch, taking care not to take the carried color through the stitch.

Knit the stitch using the right needle, dropping the stitch and the carried yarn from the left needle as you do so.

Hold the carried yarn in place at the back of the work, using your left forefinger, and continue to knit using the first color.

Continue to purl to pattern.

Weaving using both hands

This technique uses the continental method (see page 21), with one color held in each hand. This is a particularly quick and efficient way of completing Fair Isle, although it is a little more time-consuming on a purl row than on a knit row.

WEAVING ON THE RIGHT SIDE
Work to the start of the second color. Place the right needle up through the next stitch on the left needle from left to right and under the yarn on the left forefinger.

Knit the next stitch using the first color, dropping both yarns from the left needle as you do so.

Use your left forefinger to keep the carried yarn taut at the reverse of the work, and knit the next stitch.

WEAVING ON THE WRONG SIDE
Work to the point where the second color needs to be caught in. Hold the second color in place at the front of the work, using your left thumb.

Place the right needle through the next stitch from right to left and under the second yarn.

Purl the next stitch using the right needle, being careful not to push both colors through the center of the stitch. Continue to purl to pattern.

TIP

Be careful when choosing colors for Fair Isle. Heavily contrasting colors can show through to the front of the work when woven in at the back.

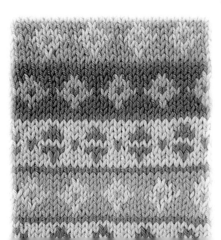

Duplicate stitch or Swiss darning

This is a way of adding small areas of color to a knitted piece once it has been completed. Duplicate stitch is worked by sewing a second color over the top of the existing knitted stitch. It is also a good way of changing colors or correcting mistakes within the piece. However, it can make the fabric quite stiff if it is used over large areas.

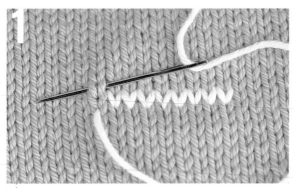

Bring the needle through the work from back to front at the base of the V shape made by a stitch.

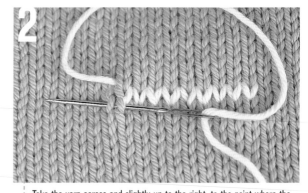

Take the yarn across and slightly up to the right, to the point where the next stitch begins. Thread the needle through both loops created by the stitch and out at the other side. Insert the needle through the piece from front to back at the point where the first stitch emerged. Bring the yarn back through the piece to the front, if required, at the base of the next stitch to the left.

This brightly striped sweater shows how different colors can work together in one garment to produce a spectacular effect

Sewing in ends

In both the intarsia and Fair Isle techniques, you will be left with ends of yarn attached to the knitted piece at the points where new colors have been added in or finished.

In the case of Fair Isle, it may be preferable (and it is certainly quicker) to weave these ends in as you work using the weaving-in technique. However, for the intarsia technique, sewing in the ends is a neater and safer alternative. To do this, remember to leave enough yarn at the beginning and end of an area of color.

Thread a knitter's sewing needle with a length of yarn and sew around the outside of the shape created by the intarsia technique, by weaving the yarn in and out of the points where the colors have been twisted in the same way as overcasting (see page 41). Pull the knitted fabric slightly to ensure that the sewn stitches have not been worked too tightly. Secure by sewing the yarn over itself a few times.

Reading a graph

Most intarsia and Fair Isle patterns are set out on a graph pattern. Graphs are read from bottom to top; read from right to left on a knit row, and from left to right on a purl row.

Some patterns are now printed in color, but those printed in black and white have a key to one side describing what colors are placed where, each color represented by a symbol of some kind.

It is a good idea to photocopy the pattern, so that you can mark off rows as you knit without ruining your master copy. Check off your work row by row as you knit, to make sure that it is correct; unpicking color work is particularly heartbreaking!

Key:

☐	Oyster 730	○	Dijon 739	✕	Passion 805
•	Mint 748	+	Delight 806	—	Sky 749

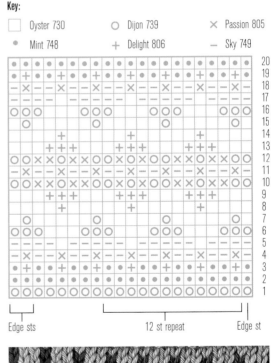

Edge sts   12 st repeat   Edge st

CHAPTER **3**
Projects

Projects

The techniques that you have learned throughout this book should now enable you to make decisions about how you can change the appearance of a garment or knitted object. You may wish to add some kind of embellishment or color feature, such as beading or intarsia, or you may decide simply to sew the piece together differently to the way the pattern suggests, thus creating knitted objects that are personal and unique.

These five basic projects, representative of the most popular areas of knitting, can be used as a starting point for countless design permutations. The projects are suitable for all knitting capabilities, and each one describes in detail the potential variations to be created using different finishing techniques. The projects have the same basic pattern according to their style, and show the kind of variations that can be achieved simply by changing a finishing technique. The objective of each project is to expand the knitter's creative horizon and give them confidence to adapt existing patterns to suit their needs and capabilities.

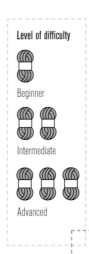

Level of difficulty

Beginner

Intermediate

Advanced

PATCHWORK CUSHION

Four knitted squares, each one in a different color, make up this cushion cover. The size of the cover can be enlarged simply by adding more knitted squares to the piece. The back of the cushion is made up of two pieces, and the cushion is fastened using Dorset buttons (see page 63).

Materials

3 x 2 oz (50 g) ball Rowan handknit cotton
    in shade 205 Linen (A)
2 x 2 oz (50 g) ball Rowan handknit cotton
    in shade 203 Fruit Salad (B)
2 x 2 oz (50 g) ball Rowan handknit cotton
    in shade 209 Artichoke (C)
2 x 2 oz (50 g) ball Rowan handknit cotton
    in shade 204 Chime (D)
1 pair size 6 (4 mm) needles
5 brass rings

Measurements

Approx 16 inches (42 cm) square.

Gauge

20 sts and 28 rows to 4 inches (10 cm) square over st st, using size 6 (4 mm) needles.

Front (make one in each color)

- With size 6 (4 mm) needles, cast on 42 sts.
- Beg with a k row, work 60 rows in st st, ending with a ws row. Bind off.

Back

- With size 6 (4 mm) needles and yarn A, cast on 60 sts. Beginning with a k row, work 2 rows st st.
- Change to yarn B and work 2 rows.
- Change to yarn C and work 2 rows.
- Change to yarn D and work 2 rows.
- Repeat sequence until the work measures 16 inches (42 cm), ending with a ws row. Bind off.

Flap

- With size 6 (4 mm) needles and yarn A, cast on 82 sts.
- **Set up row:** K1, p1 to end. Work in seed stitch (see page 22) for 6 rows.
- **Next row:** Seed st 5, p72, seed st 5.
- **Next row:** Seed st 5, k72, seed st 5.
- **Next row:** Seed st 5, p72, seed st 5.
- **Buttonhole row:** Seed st 5, k3, * yo, k2tog, k14, rep from * to last 10 sts, yo, k2tog, k3, seed st 5.
- Continue in seed st and st st as previously set, by working the five edge stitches of the flap in seed stitch and the center in stockinette stitch, until piece measures 8¾ inches (22 cm), ending with a ws row. Bind off.

Back of cushion

To finish

• Back st the four front squares together with the wrong side of the knitted fabric on the inside to create a reverse seam.

• Join back and flap to front using preferred sewing method.

• Make five Dorset buttons as described on page 63, and sew in place.

Embellished cushion

This cushion is worked in the same way as the Patchwork cushion and embellished with embroidery stitches, some sewn-on cord, and pom-poms. The measurements and gauge are the same as for the Patchwork cushion.

Materials

2 x 2 oz (50 g) ball Rowan handknit cotton
    in shade 203 Fruit Salad (A)
2 x 2 oz (50 g) ball Rowan handknit cotton
    in shade 204 Chime (B)
2 x 2 oz (50 g) ball Rowan handknit cotton
    in shade 205 Linen (C)
1 pair size 6 (4 mm) needles
1 pair size 3 (3.25 mm) needles
1 16 inch (42 cm) zipper
Contrast yarn for embroidery
Some small beads
Pom-pom maker or two cardboard disks

Front

• Work four squares as for Patchwork cushion, two yarn B and two yarn C.

Back (make two)

• With size 6 (4 mm) needles and yarn A, cast on 42 stitches.
• **Row 1 (rep throughout):** Begin seed stitch as follows: K1, * p1, k1; rep from * to end.
• Continue as set until piece measures 16 inches (42 cm) in from cast-on edge. Bind off in patt.

Flower: With size 3 (3.25 mm) needles and yarn A, cast on 6 sts. Set garter stitch thus:
• **1st row:** Knit.
• **2nd row:** Knit.
• Continue in this way working in garter st until piece measures 4 inches (10 cm).
• Cast off 3 sts and unravel remaining sts as for knitted fringe (see page 74).

To finish

• Stitch small flower motifs on two of the knitted squares.
• Using the technique as described on page 72, knit one cord measuring approx 10 inches (25 cm). Join the front squares together, using your preferred sewing technique. Overcast the knitted cord into place on the front of the cushion. Make two basic petals (see page 74) and sew into place as leaves. Curl the knitted fringe to form a circular "flower," and sew into place.
• Using chain st (see page 80), embroider a small heart shape at the center of the flower and a few more on the bottom left front of the cushion. Use an assortment of yarn in bright pink to make French knots. Sew a circular motif using chain st around the heart shapes.
• Sew the zipper in place between the two back pieces.
• Sew front to back, using your preferred sewing technique.
• Make four pom-poms 6 inches (15 cm) in diameter and attach one to each corner.

Intarsia cushion

This is a more complicated variation on the Patchwork cushion. Each square includes color work in the form of intarsia or embroidery and is completed using embroidery and beading techniques. Measurements and gauge are the same as for the Patchwork cushion.

Materials

4 x 2 oz (50 g) ball Rowan handknit cotton
in shade 205 Linen (A)
2 x 2 oz (50 g) ball Rowan handknit cotton
in shade 203 Fruit Salad (B)
2 x 2 oz (50 g) ball Rowan handknit cotton
in shade 239 Icewater (C)
2 x 2 oz (50 g) ball Rowan handknit cotton
in shade 305 Lupin (D)
2 x 2 oz (50 g) ball Rowan handknit cotton
in shade 204 Chime (E)
Contrast yarn for embroidery
Approximately 50 beads
1 pair size 6 (4 mm) needles
1 pair size 3 (3.25 mm) double-pointed needles

Front (make two)

• With size 6 (4 mm) needles and yarn A, cast on 42 sts and work 10 rows in st st beg with a k row.
• Working intarsia, work 38 rows from the chart below, ending with a ws row.
• Beg with a k row, work 10 rows in st st. Bind off.
• Make two front pieces in yarn B as for basic cushion.

Key: ☐ Yarn A   ⌄ Yarn B   • Yarn C   ○ Yarn D

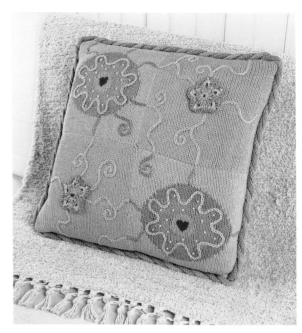

Back

• With size 6 (4 mm) needles and yarn A, cast on 82 sts. Beg with a k row, work in st st until piece measures 16 inches (42 cm) from cast-on edge, ending with a ws row. Bind off.
Knitted cord: (Make one in color C and one in color D).
• With size 3 (3.25 mm) double-pointed needles, cast on 4 sts and knit a cord approx 80 inches (200 cm) long, following the instructions on page 72.

Knitted flower: With size 6 (4 mm) needles and yarn C, cast on 57 sts.
• **1st row:** Yarn E. Purl.
• **2nd row:** Yarn D. K2 * k1, slip this stitch back onto the left needle. Pass the next 8 sts over the top of this st and off the needle. Take the yarn over the needle twice (yo twice), knit the first st again, then k2. Repeat from * to end.
• **Next row:** Yarn B. K2 tog to end.
• Purl 1 row.
• Cut yarn and, using a knitter's sewing needle, thread it through the remaining st loops and pull up to tighten. Fasten off.

To finish

• Using one of the embroidery stitches shown on pages 80–81, work around the intarsia design to create the appearance of flowers: Sew beads in place as required.
• Sew the squares together using your preferred sewing technique. Place knitted flower at center of remaining front pieces and sew into place. Use chain st to embroider swirl pattern.
• Sew front to back using preferred sewing technique.
• Twist the two knitted cords together and sew in place around the outside edge of the cushion.

 CHILD'S SWEATER

This is a simple garment with very little shaping and dropped shoulders; the only stitch detail is seed (moss) stitch on the borders, bands, and neckline. The garment could be worn by a girl or a boy. Pattern directions are for the smallest size. For medium and large sizes, follow numbers in parentheses.

Materials

5 (8:10) x 2 oz (50 g) balls Rowan wool/cotton
1 pair each size 3 (3.25 mm) and size 6 (4 mm) needles
7 (8:9) buttons

Children's Measurements

To Fit Age		
4–5	6–7	8–9
Actual Measurements		
28 ins. (71 cm)	Chest 34 ins. (86 cm)	33 ins. (40 cm)
14 ins. (36 cm)	Length to Shoulder 18 ins. (46 cm)	22 ins. (56 cm)
10 ins. (25 cm)	Sleeve Length 12 ins. (30 cm)	14 ins. (36 cm)

Gauge

22 sts and 30 rows to 4 inches (10 cm) square over st st, using size 6 (4 mm) needles.

Back

• With size 3 (3.25 mm) needles, cast on 81 (97:115) sts.
• **1st row**: K1, * p1, k1; rep from * to end.
• Rep the last row 7 (9:11) times more.
• Change to size 6 (4 mm) needles.
• Beg with a k row, cont in st st until back measures 14 (18:22) inches/36 (46:56) cm from cast-on edge, ending with a p row.

TO SHAPE SHOULDERS

• Bind off 13 (16:20) sts at beg of next 2 rows and 14 (17:20) sts at beg of foll 2 rows.
• Leave rem 27 (31:35) sts on a spare needle.

Left front

• With size 3 (3.25 mm) needles, cast on 45 (53:61) sts.
• **1st row**: K1, * p1, k1; rep from * to end.
• Rep the last row 7 (9:11) times more.
• Change to size 6 (4 mm) needles.
• **Next row**: K38 (46:54), turn, cast on 1 st, leave rem 7 sts on a holder.
Beg with a p row, cont in st st until front measures 11¾ (15:18) inches/30 (38:46) cm from cast-on edge, ending with a p row.

TO SHAPE NECK

• **Next row**: K32 (40:47), turn and work on these sts for first side of neck.
Dec 1 st at neck edge on every row until 27 (33:40) sts rem.
• Work straight until front matches back to shoulder shaping, ending at side edge.

TO SHAPE SHOULDER

• Bind off 13 (16:20) sts at beg of next row.
• Work 1 row.
• Bind off rem 14 (17:20) sts.

Right front

• With size 3 (3.25 mm) needles, cast on 45 (53:61) sts.
• **1st row, work in seed stitch**: K1, * p1, k1; rep from * to end.
• Rep the last row 3 times more.
• **Buttonhole row (right side)**: Seed st 3, work 2 tog, yo, work in seed st to end.
• Seed st 3 more rows.
• **Next row**: Seed st 7 sts, leave these sts on a holder.
• Change to size 6 (4 mm) needles.
• **Next row**: Cast on 1 st, k rem 38 (46:54) sts.
• Beg with a p row, cont in st st until front measures 11¾ (15:18) inches/30 (38:46) cm from cast-on edge, ending with a p row.

TO SHAPE NECK

• **Next row**: K7 (7:8), leave these sts on a holder, k to end, work on these sts for first side of neck.
• Dec 1 st at neck edge on every row until 27 (33:40) sts rem.
• Work straight until front matches back to shoulder shaping, ending at side edge.

TO SHAPE SHOULDER

• Bind off 13 (16:20) sts at beg of next row.
• Work 1 row.
• Bind off rem 14 (17:20) sts.

Sleeves (make two)

• With size 3 (3.25 mm) needles, cast on 51 (57:63) sts.
• Work 8 (10:12) rows seed st as given on back.
• Change to size 6 (4 mm) needles.
• Beg with a k row, cont in st st, inc 1 st at each end of the 3rd and every foll 4th row until there are 81 (95:109) sts on the needle.
• Now work straight until sleeve measures 10 (12:14) inches/25 (30:36) cm from cast-on edge, ending with a p row. Bind off.

Button band

• With size 3 (3.25 mm) needles, right side facing, join in yarn to inner edge of button band.
• **1st row**: Cast on one st, work in seed st to end.
• Cont in seed st until band fits up left front to beg of neck shaping, ending with a ws row.
• Leave sts on a holder.
• Mark positions for buttons, the first level with buttonhole on right front, the last ½ inch (1 cm) below neck edge, and the remaining 5 (6:7) spaced evenly between.

Buttonhole band

• With size 3 (3.25 mm) needles, wrong side facing, join in yarn to inner edge of buttonhole band.
• **1st row**: Cast on one st, seed st to end.
• Work as given for button band, working buttonholes, as before, to match button positions, ending with a ws row.
• Leave sts on a holder.

Neckband

• Join shoulder seams.
• Sew front bands in place.
• With size 3 (3.25 mm) needles, right side facing, (k1, p1) 3 times, work 2 tog across sts on buttonhole band, k2tog, k5 (5:6) sts from holder, pick up and k16 (20:24) sts up right side of front neck, k across 27 (31:35) sts from back neck holder, pick up and k16 (20:24) sts down left side of front neck, k5 (5:6), k2 tog, from front neck holder, work 2 tog, (k1, p1) 3 times from buttonband. 85 (97:111) sts.
• Work 7 rows in seed st.
• Bind off in seed st.

To finish

• Join sleeve seams and side seams using preferred sewing up technique.
• Sew button bands into place, and sew on buttons.

Embroidered sweater with picot edge

By making a few simple changes to the basic sweater pattern you can create a very feminine sweater suitable for a young girl. The materials, measurements, and gauge are the same as for the Child's sweater.

Back

• Work as for Child's sweater.

Pocket linings (make two)

• With size 6 (4 mm) needles, cast on 26 (28:30) sts.
• Beg with a k row, cont in st st until pocket measures 4 (4¼:4¾) inches/10 (11:12) cm from cast-on edge, ending with a p row.
• Leave these sts on a holder.

Left front

• With size 3 (3.25 mm) needles, cast on 45 (53:61) sts.

• **1st row**: K1, * p1, k1; rep from * to end.
• Rep the last row 7 (9:11) times more.
• Change to size 6 (4 mm) needles.
• **Next row**: K38 (46:54), turn, cast on 1 st, leave rem 7 sts on a holder.
• Beg with a p row, cont in st st for 4 (4¼:4¾)inches/10 (11:12) cm, ending with a p row.

TO PLACE POCKET
• **Next row**: K7 (10:13), k next 26 (28:30) and place these sts on a holder, k across sts of pocket lining, k6 (9:12).
• Cont in st st until front measures 11¾ (15:18) inches/30 (38:46) cm from cast-on edge, ending with a p row.

TO SHAPE NECK
• **Next row**: K32 (40:47), turn and work on these sts for first side of neck.
• Dec 1 st at neck edge on every row until 27 (33:40) sts rem.
• Work straight until front matches back to shoulder shaping, ending at side edge.

TO SHAPE SHOULDER
• Bind off 13 (16:20) sts at beg of next row.
• Work 1 row.
• Bind off rem 14 (17:20) sts.

Right front

• With size 3 (3.25 mm) needles, cast on 45 (53:61) sts.
• **1st row**: K1, * p1, k1; rep from * to end.
• Rep the last row 3 times more.
• **Buttonhole row (right side)**: K1, p1, k1, work 2 tog, yrn, work seed st to end.
• Work in seed st 3 more rows.
• **Next row**: K1, * p1, k1; rep from * 3 times, leave these sts on a holder.
• Change to size 6 (4 mm) needles.
• **Next row**: Cast on 1 st, k rem 38 (46:54) sts.
• Beg with a p row, cont in st st for 4 (4¼:4¾) inches/10 (11:12) cm, ending with a p row.

TO PLACE POCKET

• **Next row**: K7 (10:13), k next 26 (28:30) and place these sts on a holder, k across sts of pocket lining, k6 (9:12).
• Cont in st st until front measures 11¾ (15:18) inches/30 (38:46) cm from cast-on edge, ending with a p row.

TO SHAPE NECK

• **Next row**: K7 (7:8), leave these sts on a holder, k to end, work on these sts for first side of neck.
• Dec 1 st at neck edge on every row until 27 (33:40) sts rem.
• Work straight until front matches back to shoulder shaping, ending at side edge.

TO SHAPE SHOULDER

• Bind off 13 (16:20) sts at beg of next row.
• Work 1 row.
• Bind off rem 14 (17:20) sts.

Sleeves

• Work as for Child's sweater.

Pocket tops

• With size 3 (3.25 mm) needles, right side facing, decreasing 1 st at center, k across sts on pocket top.
• Work 3 rows seed st.
• Bind off.

Button band

• Work as for Child's sweater.

Buttonhole band

• Work as for Child's sweater.

Collar

• Join shoulder seams.
• Sew front bands in place.
• With size 3 (3.25 mm) needles, right side facing, k1, p1 3 times (seed st), work 2 tog across sts on buttonhole band, k2tog, k5 (5:6) sts from holder, pick up and k16 (20:24) sts up right side of front neck, k across 27 (31:35) sts from back neck holder, pick up and k16 (20:24) sts down left side of front neck, k5 (5:6), k2 tog from front neck holder, work 2 tog, k1, p1 3 times (seed st) from buttonband. 85 (97:111) sts.

• Cont in st st with seed st edgings.
• **Next 2 rows**: Work to last 25 (29:33) sts, turn.
• **Next 2 rows**: Work to last 21 (24:27) sts, turn.
• **Next 2 rows**: Work to last 17 (19:21) sts, turn.
• **Next 2 rows**: Work to last 13 (14:15) sts, turn.
• **Next 2 rows**: Work to last 7 sts, turn.
• Work to end.
• Bind off 4 sts at beg of next 2 rows.
• **Next row**: Seed st, 3, k to last 3 sts, seed st 3.
• **Next row**: Seed st, 3, p to last 3 sts, seed st 3.
• Rep the last 2 rows 7 (8:9) times more.
• Work 4 rows in seed st.
• Bind off in seed st.

Sleeve edging

• With size 3 (3.25 mm) needles, right side facing, pick up and bind off at the same time as folls:
• Pick up and k2 sts, bind off knitwise 1 st, * slip st used in binding off back onto left-hand needle, cast on 2 sts knitwise, bind off 2 sts knitwise, [pick up and k 1 st, bind off knitwise 1 st] 4 times, rep from * to end. Fasten off.

Pocket edging and lower edging

• Work as for sleeve edging.

Collar edging

• Working along short sides and outside edge of collar, work as for sleeve edging.

To finish

• Sew on sleeves. Join side and sleeve seams. Sew down pocket linings and pocket tops. Sew on buttons.
• Using embroidery stitches as shown on pages 80–81, work an embroidered flower and stem. Work a small petal motif on the edge of the collar. Sew beads in place around collar and pocket tops and on flower stem.

Boy's sweater with intarsia detail

A patch pocket with color detail and knitted cords used as ties have been added to the basic sweater design to give it a more masculine feel. Measurements and gauge are the same as for the Child's sweater.

Materials

5 (8:10) x 2 oz (50 g) balls Rowan wool/cotton in rich shade main 911 (M)

1 x 2 oz (50 g) balls Rowan wool/cotton in navy shade contrast 909 (C)

1 pair size 5 (3.25 mm) needles

1 pair size 6 (4 mm) needles

1 pair size 5 (3.25 mm) double-pointed needles

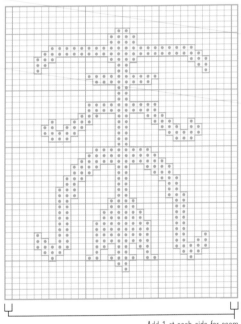

Key:

☐ Yarn M

• Yarn C

Add 1 st each side for seam

Back

• With size 3 (3.25 mm) needles and M (main color), cast on 82 (98:114) sts.
• **Set rib**: K2M, *k2C, k2M; rep from * to end.
• **1st rib row**: P2M, * k2C, p2M; rep from * to end.
• **2nd rib row**: K2M, * p2C, k2M; rep from * to end.
• Rep the last 2 rows 4 (5:6) times more.
• Change to size 6 (4 mm) needles.
• Using M only, beg with a k row, cont in st st until back measures 14 (18:22) inches/36 (46:56) cm from cast-on edge, ending with a p row.

TO SHAPE SHOULDERS

• Bind off 13 (16:20) sts at beg of next 2 rows and 14 (17:20) sts at beg of foll 2 rows.
• Leave rem 28 (32:34) sts on a spare needle.

Left front

• With size 3 (3.25 mm) needles and M, cast on 45 (53:61) sts.
• Set rib: K2M, * k2C, k2M; rep from * to end.
• **1st rib row**: P2M, * k2C, p2M; rep from * to end.
• **2nd rib row**: K2M, * p2C, k2M; rep from * to end **.
• **Buttonhole row (right side)**: Seed st 3, yo, work 2 tog, seed st 2, patt to end.
• Patt 4 more rows.
• Change to size 6 (4 mm) needles and M.
• **Next row**: K38 (46:54), turn, cast on 1 st, leave rem 7 sts on a holder.
• Beg with a p row, cont in st st until front measures 11¾ (15:18) inches/30 (38:48) cm from cast-on edge, ending with a p row.

TO SHAPE NECK

• **Next row**: K32 (40:47), turn and work on these sts for first side of neck.
• Dec 1 st at neck edge on every row until 27 (33:40) sts rem.
• Work straight until front matches back to shoulder shaping, ending at side edge.

TO SHAPE SHOULDER

• Bind off 13 (16:20) sts at beg of next row.
• Work 1 row.
• Bind off rem 14 (17:20) sts.

Right front

• Work as for left front to **.
• Repeat last 2 rows 3 (4:5) times.
• Repeat 1st row again.
• **Next row**: Seed st 7 sts, leave these sts on a holder.
• Change to size 6 (4 mm) needles and cont in M only.
• **Next row**: Cast on 1 st, k rem 38 (46:54) sts.
• Beg with a p row, cont in st st until front measures 11¾ (15:18) inches /30 (38:48) cm from cast-on edge, ending with a p row.

TO SHAPE NECK

• **Next row**: K7 (7:8), leave these sts on a holder, k to end, work on these sts for first side of neck.
• Dec 1 st at neck edge on every row until 27 (33:40) sts rem.
• Work straight until front matches back to shoulder shaping, ending at side edge.

TO SHAPE SHOULDER

- Bind off 13 (16:20) sts at beg of next row.
- Work 1 row.
- Bind off rem 14 (17:20) sts.

Sleeves

- With size 3 (3.25 mm) needles and M, cast on 50 (54:62) sts.
- Set rib k2M, * k2C, k2M; rep from * to end.
- **1st rib row**: P2M, * k2C, p2M; rep from * to end.
- **2nd rib row**: K2M, * p2C, k2M; rep from * to end.
- Rep the last 2 rows 3 (4:5) times.
- Rep 1st row again.
- Change to size 6 (4 mm) needles.
- Beg with a k row, cont in st st, inc 1 st at each end of the 3rd and every foll 4th row until there are 80 (92:108) sts on the needle.
- Now work straight until sleeve measures 10 (12:14) inches/25 (30:36) cm from cast-on edge, ending with a p row.
- Bind off.

Pocket

- With size 6 (4 mm) needles and M, cast on 32 sts.
- Starting with a k row, work in patt from chart using the intarsia technique.
- Change to size 3 (3.25 mm) needles.
- Work 4 rows seed st.
- Bind off in seed st.

Button band

- With size 3 (3.25 mm) needles, right side facing, join in yarn to inner edge of button band.
- **1st row**: Cast on 1 st, work in seed st to end.
- Cont in seed st until band fits up left front to beg of neck shaping, ending with a ws row.
- Leave sts on a holder.
- Mark positions for buttons, the first level with buttonhole on right front, the last ½ inch (1 cm) below neck edge, and the remaining 5 (6:7) spaced evenly between.

Buttonhole band

- With size 3 (3.25 mm) needles, wrong side facing, join in yarn to inner edge of buttonhole band.
- **1st row**: Cast on 1 st, work in seed st to end.
- Work as given for button band, working buttonholes, as before, to match button positions, ending with a ws row.
- Leave sts on a holder.

Collar

- Join shoulder seams.
- Sew front bands in place.
- With size 3 (3.25 mm) needles, right side facing, seed st 6, work 2 tog across sts on buttonhole band, k2tog, k5 (5:6) sts from holder, pick up and k16 (20:24) sts up right side of front neck, decreasing 1 (1:3) sts, k across 27 (31:35) sts from back neck holder, pick up and k16 (20:24) sts down left side of front neck, k5 (5:6), k2 tog, from front neck holder, work 2 tog, seed st 6 from buttonband. 84 (96:108) sts.
- **Next row**: With M bind off 6, then p2M, * k2C, p2M; rep from * to last 7 sts, with M seed st 7.
- **Next row**: With M bind off 6, then k2M, * p2C, k2M; rep from * to last st, with M seed st 1.
- Keeping edge st in seed st, work a further 7 rows in rib as set.
- Using M, k 1 row.
- Bind off.

Cords (make four)

- With two double-pointed size 3 (3.25 mm) needles and M shade, cast on 4 sts.
- K 1 row, do not turn * now bring yarn tightly across back of work, k4; rep from * until cord measures 6 inches (15 cm). Fasten off.

To finish

- Sew on sleeves. Join side and sleeve seams. Sew on buttons. Sew pocket in place. Sew on cords at neck edge.

WOMAN'S SWEATER WITH LACY BORDER

This is a fitted woman's sweater with full fashioning as a design feature. The sweater is gently shaped at the waistline and has lace edging on the sleeves and cuffs.

Materials

12 (13:14) balls of Rowan Glace Cotton Mint 748
1 pair each size 2 (3 mm) and size 3 (3.25 mm) needles
Long circular size 2 (3 mm) and size 3 (3.25 mm) needle
14 buttons

Women's Measurements

To Fit Bust		
34 ins. (86 cm)	36 ins. (92 cm)	38 ins. (97 cm)
Actual Measurements		
38 ins. (96 cm)	Bust 40 ins. (101 cm)	42 ins. (106 cm)
21 ins. (53 cm)	Length to Shoulder 21½ ins. (54 cm)	22 ins. (56 cm)
19 ins. (48 cm)	Sleeve Length 19¼ ins. (49 cm)	19¾ ins. (54 cm)

Gauge

23 sts and 32 rows to 4 inches (10 cm) square over st st, using size 3 (3.25 mm) needles.

Back

- With size 2 (3 mm) needles, cast on 112 (118:124) sts.
- K 4 rows.
- Change to size 3 (3.25 mm) needles.
- Beg with a k row, work 16 rows in st st.
- **1st dec row**: K26 (28:30), skp, k1, k2 tog, k50 (52:54), skp, k1, k2 tog, k26 (28:30). 108 (114:120) sts.
- St st 5 rows straight.
- **2nd dec row**: K25 (27:29), skp, k1, k2 tog, k48 (50:52), skp, k1, k2 tog, k25 (27:29). 104 (110:116) sts.
- St st 5 rows straight.
- **3rd dec row**: K24 (26:28), skp, k1, k2 tog, k46 (48:50), skp, k1, k2 tog, k24 (26:28). 100 (106:112) sts.

- St st 5 rows straight.
- Cont to dec in this way on next and every foll 6th row until 80 (86:92) sts rem.
- St st 3 (5:7) rows straight.
- **1st inc row**: K19 (21:23), m1, k1, m1, k36 (38:40), m1, k1, m1, k19 (21:23). 84 (90:96) sts.
- St st 3 rows.
- **2nd inc row**: K20 (22:24), m1, k1, m1, k38 (40:42), m1, k1, m1, k20 (22:24). 88 (94:100) sts.
- St st 3 rows.
- Cont to inc in this way on the next and every foll 4th row until there are 112 (118:124) sts.
- Cont in st st until back measures 14 (14:14½) inches/36 (36:37) cm from cast-on edge, ending with a ws row.

TO SHAPE ARMHOLES

- Bind off 7 (8:9) sts at beg of next 2 rows.
- Dec 1 st at each end of next and every foll alt row until 90 (94:98) sts rem.
- Cont in st st until back measures 21 (21½:22) inches/53 (54:56) cm from cast-on edge, ending with a ws row.

TO SHAPE BACK NECK AND SHOULDERS

- **Next row**: K30 (32:34) sts, turn and work on these sts for first side of neck shaping.
- **Next row**: Bind off 3 sts, p to end.
- **Next row**: Bind off 8 (9:10) sts, k to end.
- **Next row**: Bind off 2 sts, p to end.
- **Next row**: Bind off 8 (9:10) sts, st st to end.
- **Next row**: Patt to end.
- **Next row**: Bind off rem 9 sts.
- With right side facing, rejoin yarn to rem sts, bind off 30 sts, k to end.
- Complete to match first side.

Left front

- With size 2 (3 mm) needles and M, cast on 54 (57:60) sts.
- K 4 rows.
- Change to size 3 (3.25 mm) needles.
- Beg with a k row, work 16 rows in st st.
- **1st dec row**: K26 (28:30), skp, k1, k2 tog, k23 (24:25). 52 (55:58) sts.
- St st 5 rows straight.
- **2nd dec row**: K25 (27:29), skp, k1, k2 tog, k22 (23:24). 50 (53:56) sts.
- St st 5 rows straight.
- **3rd dec row**: K24 (26:28), skp, k1, k2 tog, k21 (22:23). 48 (51:54) sts.
- St st 5 rows straight.

• Cont to dec in this way on next and every foll 6th row until 38 (41:44) sts rem.

• St st 3 (5:7) rows straight.

• **1st inc row**: K19 (21:23), m1, k1, m1, k16 (17:18). 40 (43:46) sts.

• St st 3 rows.

• **2nd inc row**: K20 (22:24), m1, k1, m1, k17 (18:19). 42 (45:48) sts.

• St st 3 rows.

• Cont to inc in this way on the next and every foll 4th row until there are 54 (57:60) sts.

• Cont in st st until front measures 14 (14:14½) inches/36 (36:37) cm from cast-on edge, ending with a ws row.

TO SHAPE ARMHOLE

• Bind off 7 (8:9) sts at beg of next row.

• Work 1 row.

• Dec 1 st at armhole edge of next and every foll alt row until 43 (45:47) sts rem.

• Cont in st st until front measures 18½ (19:19¼) inches/47 (48:49) cm from cast-on edge, ending with a ws row.

TO SHAPE FRONT NECK

• **Next row**: K to last 8 (9:10) sts, turn and leave rem sts on a holder.

• Dec 1 st at neck edge on every row until 25 (27:29) sts rem.

• Work straight until front matches back to shoulder shaping, ending at armhole edge.

TO SHAPE SHOULDER

• Bind off 8 (9:10) sts, at beg of next and foll alt row.

• Work 1 row.

• Next row: Bind off rem 9 sts.

Right front

• With size 2 (3 mm) needles and M, cast on 54 (57:60) sts.

• K 4 rows.

• Change to size 3 (3.25 mm) needles.

• Beg with a k row, work 16 rows in st st.

• **1st dec row**: K23 (24:25), skp, k1, k2 tog, k26 (28:30). 52 (55:58) sts.

• St st 5 rows straight.

• **2nd dec row**: K22 (23:24), skp, k1, k2 tog, k25 (27:29). 50 (53:56) sts.

• St st 5 rows straight.

• **3rd dec row**: K21 (22:23), skp, k1, k2 tog, k24 (26:28). 48 (51:54) sts.

• Work st st for 5 rows straight.

• Cont to dec in this way on next and every foll 6th row until 38 (41:44) sts rem.

• Work st st for 3 (5:7) rows straight.

• **1st inc row**: K16 (17:18), m1, k1, m1, k19 (21:23). 40 (43:46) sts.

• Work st st for 3 rows.

• **2nd inc row:** K17 (18:19), m1, k1, m1, k20 (22:24). 42 (45:48) sts.

• Work st st for 3 rows.

• Cont to inc in this way on the next and every foll 4th row until there are 54 (57:60) sts.

• Cont in st st until front measures 14 (14:14½) inches/36 (36:37) cm from cast-on edge, ending with a rs row.

TO SHAPE ARMHOLE

• Bind off 7 (8:9) sts at beg of next row.
• Dec 1 st at armhole edge of next and every foll alt row until 43 (45:47) sts rem.
• Cont in st st until front measures 18½ (19:19¼) inches/47 (48:49) cm from cast-on edge, ending with a ws row.

TO SHAPE FRONT NECK

• **Next row**: K8 (9:10) sts, leave sts on a holder, k to end.
• Dec 1 st at neck edge on every row until 25 (27:29) sts rem.
• Work straight until front matches back to shoulder shaping, ending at armhole edge.

TO SHAPE SHOULDER

• Bind off 8 (9:10) sts, at beg of next and foll alt row.
• Work 1 row.
• Next row: Bind off rem 9 sts.

Sleeves

• With size 2 (3 mm) needles, cast on 44 (48:52) sts.
• K 4 rows.
• Change to size 3 (3.25 mm) needles.
• Beg with a k row, cont in st st inc 1 st at each end of the 3rd and every foll 8th row until there are 76 (80:84) sts.
• Work straight in st st until sleeve measures 16½ (17:17¼) inches/42 (43:44) cm from cast-on edge, ending with a p row.

TO SHAPE SLEEVE TOP

• Bind off 7 (8:9) sts at beg of next 2 rows.
• Dec 1 st at each end of the next and every foll alt row until 40 (42:44) sts rem.
• Now dec 1 st at each end of every foll 4th row until 34 sts rem.
• Work 1 row.
• Dec 1 st at each end of next and foll alt rows.
• Dec 1 st at each end of next 5 rows.
• Bind off 3 sts at beg of next 2 rows.
• Bind off rem 14 sts.

Sleeve border (make two)

• With size 3 (3.25 mm) needles, cast on 17 sts.
• **1st row**: K3, yo, p2tog, yo, p2tog, yo, k1 tbl, k2 tog, p1, yb, skp, k1 tbl, yo k3.
• **2nd row**: K3, p3, k1, p3, k2, yo, p2tog, yo, p2tog, k1.
• **3rd and 4th rows**: As 1st and 2nd rows.
• **5th row**: K3, yo, p2tog, yo, p2 tog, yo, k1 tbl, yb, k2 tog, p1, yo, skp, yo, k4. 18 sts.
• **6th row**: K4, p2, k1, p4, k2, yo, p2tog, yo, p2tog, k1.

• **7th row**: K3, yo, p2tog, yo, p2tog, yo, k1 tbl, k1, k1 tbl, yo, sl 1, k2tog, psso, yo, k5. 19 sts.
• **8th row**: K5, p7, k2, yo, p2tog, yo, p2tog, k1.
• **9th row**: K3, yo, p2tog, yo, p2tog, yo, k1 tbl, k3, k1 tbl, yo, k7. 21 sts.
• **10th row**: Bind off 4 sts, k2, p7, k2, yo, p2tog, yo, p2tog, k1. 17 sts.
• Rep 1st to 10th rows until border fits along lower edge.
• Bind off.
• Sew straight edge of border to cast-on edge of sleeves.

Lower border

• Join side seams.
• Work as given for sleeve border until straight edge fits along lower edge of jacket, ending row 10.
• Bind off.
• Sew straight edge of border to cast-on edges of fronts and back.

Neck border

• With size 2 (3 mm) needles and right side facing, slip 8 (9:10) sts from holder onto a needle, pick up and k27 sts up right side of front neck, 7 sts down right side of back neck, k30 sts from back neck holder, pick up and k7 sts up left back neck, 27 sts down left front neck, k8 (9:10) sts from front neck holder.
• K5 rows.
• Bind off.

Buttonhole band

• With size 2 (3 mm) needles and right side facing, pick up and k135 sts along front edge to beg of neck shaping.
• K 1 row.
• Buttonhole row k1, [k2 tog, yo, k8 sts] 13 times, k2 tog, yo, k2.
• K 2 rows.
• Bind off.

Button band

• With size 2 (3 mm) needles and right side facing, starting at neck shaping, pick up and k135 sts along front edge.
• K 4 rows.
• Bind off.

To finish

• Join sleeve seams. Sew on sleeves. Sew on buttons.

Sweater with Fair Isle border

This sweater has the same number of stitches and is the same length as the Woman's sweater with lacy border, but it is not shaped at the waistline. The Fair Isle bands and collar give this garment its interest. The measurements and gauge are the same as for the Woman's sweater with lacy border.

Materials

11 (11:12) x 20 oz (50 g) balls of main color—Rowan Glace Cotton in shade Sky 649 (M), and 2 balls each in Passion 805, Mint 748, Oyster 730, Dijon 739, and Delight 806.
1 pair each of size 2 (3 mm) and size 3 (3.25 mm) needles
Long circular size 2 (3 mm) and size 3 (3.25 mm) needles
9 buttons

Charts

When working from charts, the odd rows are knit rows and are read from right to left, while the even rows are purl rows and are read from left to right. When working in pattern, strand the yarn that is not in use loosely across the wrong side to keep the fabric elastic, weaving in if necessary.

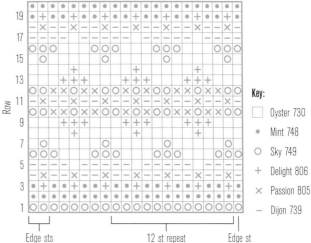

Key:

☐ Oyster 730
• Mint 748
○ Sky 749
+ Delight 806
× Passion 805
— Dijon 739

Edge sts   12 st repeat   Edge st

Back

- With size 2 (3 mm) and M, cast on 112 (118:124) sts.
- K 4 rows.
- Change to size 3 (3.25 mm) needles.
- Beg with a k row, cont in st st until back measures 14 (14:14½) inches/36 (36:37) cm from cast-on edge, ending with a ws row.

TO SHAPE ARMHOLES

• Bind off 7 (8:9) sts at beg of next 2 rows.
• Dec 1 st at each end of next and every foll alt row until 90 (94:98) sts rem.
• Cont in st st until back measures 21 (21½:22) inches/53 (54:56) cm from cast-on edge, ending with a ws row.

TO SHAPE BACK NECK AND SHOULDERS

• Next row: K30 (32:34) sts, turn and work on these sts for first side of neck shaping.
• **Next row**: Bind off 3 sts, p to end.
• **Next row**: Bind off 8 (9:10) sts, k to end.
• **Next row**: Bind off 2 sts, p to end.
• **Next row**: Bind off 8 (9:10) sts, k to end.
• **Next row**: St st to end.
• **Next row**: Bind off rem 9 sts.
• With right side facing, rejoin yarn to rem sts, bind off 30 sts, k to end.
• Complete to match first side.

Left front

• With size 2 (3 mm) needles and M, cast on 54 (57:60) sts.
• K 4 rows.
• Change to size 3 (3.25 mm) needles.
• Beg with a k row, cont in st st until back measures 14 (14:14½) inches/36 (36:37) cm from cast-on edge, ending with a ws row.

TO SHAPE ARMHOLE

• Bind off 7 (8:9) sts at beg of next row.
• Work 1 row.
• Dec 1 st at armhole edge of next and every foll alt row until 43 (45:47) sts rem.
• Cont in st st until front measures 15½ (16:16½) inches/40 (41:42) cm from cast-on edge, ending with a ws row.

TO SHAPE FRONT NECK

• **Next row**: Dec 1 st at neck edge on next and every foll alt row until 31 (33:35) sts remain, then every foll 3rd row until 25 (27:29) sts rem.
• Work straight until front matches back to shoulder shaping, ending at armhole edge.

TO SHAPE SHOULDER

• Bind off 8 (9:10) sts, at beg of next and foll alt row.
• Work 1 row.
• **Next row**: Bind off rem 9 sts.

Right front

• With size 2 (3 mm) needles and M, cast on 54 (57:60) sts.

• K 4 rows.
• Change to size 3 (3.25 mm) needles.
• Beg with a k row, cont in st st until back measures 14 (14:14½) inches/36 (36:37) cm from cast-on edge, ending with a ws row.

TO SHAPE ARMHOLE

• Bind off 7 (8:9) sts at beg of next row.
• Dec 1 st at armhole edge of next and every foll alt row until 43 (45:47) sts rem.
• Cont in st st until front measures 15½ (16:16½) inches/40 (41:42) cm from cast-on edge, ending with a ws row.

TO SHAPE FRONT NECK

• Dec 1 st at neck edge on next and every foll alt row until 31 (33:35) sts remain, then every foll 3rd row until 25 (27:29) sts rem.
• Work straight until front matches back to shoulder shaping, ending at armhole edge.

TO SHAPE SHOULDER

• Bind off 8 (9:10) sts, at beg of next and foll alt row.
• Work 1 row.
• Next row: Bind off rem 9 sts.

SLEEVES

• With size 2 (3 mm) needles and M, cast on 44 (46:50) sts.
• K 4 rows.
• Change to size 3 (3.25 mm) needles.
• Beg with a k row, cont in st st, inc 1 st at each end of the 3rd and every foll 8th row until there are 76 (80:84) sts.
• Cont straight until sleeve measures 16½ (17:17¼) inches/42 (43:44) cm from cast-on edge, ending with a p row.

TO SHAPE SLEEVE TOP

• Bind off 7 (8:9) sts at beg of next 2 rows.
• Dec 1 st at each end of the next and every foll alt row until 40 (42:44) sts rem.
• Now dec 1 st at each end of every foll 4th row until 34 sts rem.
• Work 1 row.
• Dec 1 st at each end of next and foll alt row.
• Dec 1 st at each end of next 5 rows.
• Bind off 3 sts at beg of next 2 rows.
• Bind off rem 14 sts.

Lower border

• Join side seams.
• With size 3 (3.25 mm) circular needle, right side facing, and with M, pick up and k213 (225:237) sts evenly along lower edge.

- Starting with a p row and beg at row 2, work in patt from chart to end of row 20.
- Change to size 2 (3 mm) circular needle.
- Cont in M.
- K 5 rows.
- Bind off.

Sleeve border

- With size 3 (3.25 mm) needles, right side facing, and M, pick up and k45 sts evenly along lower edge.
- Starting with a p row and beg at row 2, work in patt from chart to the end of row 6.
- Change to size 2 (3 mm) needles.
- Cont in M.
- K 5 rows.
- Bind off.

Buttonhole band

- With size 2 (3 mm) needles and right side facing, pick up and k104 sts along front edge to beg of neck shaping.
- K 1 row.
- **Buttonhole row**: K1, [k2 tog, yo, k7 sts] 11 times, k2 tog, yo, k2.
- K 2 rows.
- Bind off.

Button band

- With size 2 (3 mm) needles, right side facing, and M, starting at neck shaping, pick up and k104 sts along front edge.
- K 4 rows.
- Bind off.

Collar

- Join shoulder seams.
- With size 3 (3.25 mm) needles, wrong side facing, and M, starting at beg of neck shaping, pick up and k42 sts up neck edge to shoulder, 7 sts down left side of back neck, 31 sts across back neck, 7 sts up right side of back neck, 42 sts down neck edge to beg of neck shaping. (129 sts).
- Beg with a p row, cont in st st.
- **Next 2 rows**: Work to last 39 sts, turn.
- **Next 2 rows**: Work to last 36 sts, turn.
- **Next 2 rows**: Work to last 33 sts, turn.
- **Next 2 rows**: Work to last 30 sts, turn.
- **Next 2 rows**: Work to last 27 sts, turn.
- Continue in this way working 3 less sts on every row until 15 sts remain unworked at each end of row.

- Work last 6 rows from chart.
- **Next 2 rows**: Work to last 9 sts, turn.
- **Next 2 rows**: Work to last 6 sts, turn.
- **Next 2 rows**: Work to last 3 sts, turn.
- Work to end.
- P 4 rows increasing 1 st at each end of every row.
- Bind off.

To finish

- Join sleeve seams. Sew in sleeves. Sew on buttons. Sew row ends of collar to buttonholes and button band.

Changing colors

It is surprising how much you can change the appearance of a Fair Isle design, simply by choosing an alternative background color or by swapping two colors and working one in place of the other. In the following examples only two colors have been swapped.

Sky 749 has been swapped with Dijon 730

Sky 749 has been swapped with Passion 805

Sky 749 has been swapped with Oyster 730

SMALL SHOULDER BAG WITH FLAP DETAIL

This is a simple pattern to follow and is designed with the novice knitter in mind. The bag itself is stockinette stitch with a twisted cord strap and a knitted flap.

Knitting a bag or purse was a favorite pastime at the turn of the last century. Made using fine yarns, color, and beading work, these simple purses are based on a knitted rectangle, giving you three alternative design options.

Materials

1 x 2 oz (50 g) ball Jaeger Matchmaker 4-ply in shade 741 Mineral
1 pair size 2 (3 mm) needles

Measurements

5 inches (14 cm) wide by 7 inches (18 cm) long.

Gauge

28 sts and 36 rows to 4 inches (10 cm) square over st st, using size 2 (3 mm) needles.

Front

• With size 2 (3 mm) needles, cast on 44 sts.
• Beg with a k row, work in st st until piece measures 7 inches (18 cm) from cast-on edge, ending with a ws row.
• Bind off.

Back

• With size 2 (3 mm) needles, pick up and k44 sts along the cast-on edge of front. Knit one row. Beginning with a k row, continue in st st and work as for front.
• Transfer all sts to a holder or spare needle.

Flap

• With size 2 (3 mm) needles, cast on 8 sts.
• K 1 row.
• P 1 row.
• Next row, begin increase:
• **Row 1**: K2, yo, k4, yo, k2.
• **Row 2**: P2, yo, p6, yo, p2.

• **Row 3**: K2, yo, k8, yo, k2.
• **Row 4**: P2, yo, p10, yo, p2.
• Cont to increase in this way, working all new sts into st st until 44 sts.
• Work 6 rows st st.
• Transfer all stitches to a holder or spare needle.

Strap

• Make a twisted loop approximately 32 inches (80 cm) long, using four ends of yarn and the technique as described in Embellishments, page 73.

Button loop

• Make a sewn button loop as described in Buttons and Buttonholes, page 67, at the bottom edge of the knitted flap.

To finish

• Bind off the sts for back and the sts for flap together using three needle bind-off (see page 49) with wrong sides facing to create a reverse seam.
• Join side seams using your preferred sewing technique.
• Sew button loop in place at bottom of flap and sew strap in place.

Variations

You can change the appearance of the bag by making a few basic alterations to the knitted flap.

Sew a row of buttons along the bottom edge of the flap, or in patterns to create button "flowers"

Sew a twisted cord in two colors onto the edge of the flap

Make a small flower and sew it to the flap of the bag

Drawstring coin bag with Fair Isle detail

This could be used as a small evening purse and is ideal for carrying loose change and make-up. Line it with a piece of silk fabric to add a touch of glamor.

For a simple variation, swap the two colors and use B as the main and A as the second color.

Materials

1 x 2 oz (50 g) ball Jaeger 4-ply silk in shade 136 Midnight (A)
1 x 2 oz (50 g) ball Jaeger 4-ply silk in shade 131 Silver Blue (B)
1 pair size 2 (3 mm) knitting needles
66 gunmetal beads

Measurements

5 inches (14 cm) wide by 7 inches (19 cm) long.

Gauge

28 sts and 38 rows to 4 inches (10 cm) square over st st, using size 2 (3 mm) needles.

Front

• With size 2 (3 mm) needles and yarn B, cast on 44 sts.
• Beg with a k row, work 4 rows in st st.
• ** Using the Fair Isle technique, work 4 rows from chart (see page 115).
• Using yarn A only, continue in st st until piece measures 5 inches (14.5 cm) from cast-on edge, ending with a ws row.
• Bind off.

Back

• With size 3 (3 mm) needles and yarn B, pick up and k 44 stitches along cast-on edge of front.
• Beg with a p row, work 3 rows in st st, then complete to match front from **.

Lacy garter stitch edging

• Thread 42 beads onto yarn A (see page 76). With size 2 (3 mm) needles and yarn A, cast on 10 sts. (Note that the number of sts will change from row to row and should only be counted after the 8th row.)

• **Row 1**: K3, (yo, k2tog) twice, (yo) twice, k2tog, k1.
• **Row 2**: K3, p1, k2, (yo, k2tog) twice, k1.
• **Row 3**: K3, (yo, k2tog) twice, k1, (yo) twice, k2 tog, k1.
• **Row 4**: K3, p1, k3, (yo, k2tog) twice, k1.
• **Row 5**: K3, (yo, k2tog) twice, k2, (yo) twice, k2 tog, k1.
• **Row 6**: K3, p1, k4, (yo, k2tog) twice, k1.
• **Row 7**: K3, (yo, k2tog) twice, k6.
• **Row 8**: Bring three beads up the yarn to the needle and, holding them in place, bind off 3 sts, k4 (not including stitch left on needle after bind-off), (yo, k2tog) twice, k1.
• Repeat the 8-row pattern 13 times more. Purl 1 row, turn, and bind off.

Twisted cord

• With yarn B, make a twisted cord approx. 31 inches (80 cm) long (see page 72).
• Knot both ends, leaving the yarn ends approx. 3 inches (8 cm) long. Thread three beads onto each yarn end and knot to secure.

To finish

• Join front and back seams, using mattress stitch or your preferred sewing technique.
• Slip stitch the edging in place along the top edge of the bag, joining the cast-on edge to the bound-off edge.
• Thread the twisted cord through the first eyelet row created by the lacy garter stitch edging.

Beaded handbag

The method of beading used in this project places the bead using a slip stitch. The beads are placed every alternate stitch, so an odd number of stitches is required for the pattern to work.

The bag requires a large number of beads and it is best to thread these on in batches, maybe after each color change. Remember that the beads you thread on last are the ones that you use to knit first. You can use just one color of bead if you prefer.

Materials

1 x 2 oz (50 g) ball Jaeger Siena 4-ply in shade 415 Arctic
1 pair size 2 (3 mm) needles
Approx 400 beads in each of three colors
Small buckle

Measurements

6 inches (15 cm) wide by 5 inches (12 cm) long.

Gauge

28 sts and 38 rows to 4 inches (10 cm) square over st st, using size 2 (3 mm) needles.

Special abbreviation

b1 = bead one. Bring the bead to the top of the yarn level with the needles. Bring the yarn forward between the two needles and hold the bead at the front. Slip the next st purlwise and take the yarn to the back through the needles.

Front and back

• Using the technique described on page 76, thread the beads onto the yarn in this order:
143 light blue
(1 blue, 3 light blue) 5 times
(2 blue, 2 light blue) 5 times
(3 blue, 1 light blue) 5 times
145 blue
(1 green, 3 blue) 5 times
(2 green, 2 blue) 5 times
(3 green, 1 blue) 5 times
145 green
• With size 2 (3 mm) needles,

cast on 45 sts.
• K 1 row.
• P 1 row.
• **Next row**: K3, * b1, k1. Rep from * to last 4 sts, b1, k3.
• **Next and every alternate row**: P.
• **Next row**: K2, * b1, k1. Rep from * to last 3 sts, b1, k2.
• These 4 rows set the pattern and are repeated 12 times.
• Work first beading row again.
• P 3 rows.
• Beg with a k row, work 6 rows st st. Bind off.

Buckle band

• Thread 72 beads of choice onto yarn.
• Cast on 31 sts and work 3 rows st st, beg with a k row.
• K 2 rows to form turning ridge.
• P 1 row.
• **Next row**: K2, * b1, k1, rep from * to last st k1.
• **Next and every alternate row**: Purl.
• **Next row**: K1, * b1, k1 rep from * to end.
• Repeat these for rows once more, then repeat first beading row again.
• P 3 rows.
• K 1 row.
• P 1 row.
• Bind off.

Handle

• Make a knitted cord or i-cord. Using two size 2 (3 mm) double-pointed needles, cast on 4 sts and work a cord approx 13 inches (33 cm) long, or to the length required (see page 72).

To finish

• Join front and back seams, using your preferred sewing technique, and stitch hem in place.
• Sew front and back cast-on edges together, using back stitch to form an edge for fringing.
• Fold buckle band along turning ridges and slip stitch cast-on and bind-off edges together. Sew in place at center of top edge of bag.
• Sew in position just inside top edge of bag.
• Sew buckle in place on front.

Fringing

• Thread two beads of each color used onto 45 pieces of yarn approximately 8 inches (20 cm) long and knot both ends. Using a crochet hook, pull a strand of yarn through the center of each st along the bottom edge of both sides of the bag simultaneously, and pass the yarn ends through the loop created. Gently pull to tighten.

MAN'S SWEATER WITH SEED STITCH BORDERS

This garment uses an Aran, or fisherman weight, of yarn and is simple in design. The only stitch detailing is seed stitch, with a simple patch pocket as a small design feature.

Materials

18 (19:20) x 2 oz (50 g) balls Jaeger Matchmaker Merino Aran in shade 629 Mariner
1 pair each size 6 (4 mm) and size 7 (4.5 mm) needles
3 buttons

Men's Measurements

To Fit Chest		
40 ins. (102 cm)	42 ins. (107 cm)	44 ins. (112 cm)
Actual Measurements		
	Chest	
50 ins. (127 cm)	52 ins. (132 cm)	54 ins. (137 cm)
	Length to Shoulder	
24¾ ins. (63 cm)	25½ ins. (65 cm)	26½ ins. (67 cm)
	Sleeve Length	
21 ins. (54 cm)	21¼ ins. (55 cm)	22 ins. (56 cm)

Gauge

19 sts and 25 rows to 4 inches (10 cm) square over st st, using size 7 (4.5 mm) needles.

Back

• With size 6 (4 mm) needles, cast on 121 (127:133) sts.
• **1st row**: k1, * p1, k1; rep from * to end.
• Rep the last row for 2½ inches (6 cm).
• Change to size 7 (4.5 mm) needles.
• Beg with a k row, cont in st st until back measures 22½ (23:24) inches/ 57 (59:61) cm from cast-on edge, ending with a p row.
• Change to size 6 (4 mm) needles.
• Work a further ¾ inch (2 cm) in seed st, ending with a ws row.

TO SHAPE NECK

• **Next row**: K 44 (46:48) sts, turn and work on these sts for first side of neck.
• Dec 1 st at neck edge on next 2 rows.
• Work 1 row.

TO SHAPE SHOULDER

• Bind off 20 (21:22) sts at beg of next row.
• Work 1 row.
• Bind off rem 20 (21:22) sts.
• With right side facing, slip next 33 (35:37) sts on a spare needle, rejoin yarn to next st, k to end.
• Complete to match first side.

Front

• Work as for back until front measures 21½ (22½:23) inches/55 (57:59) cm from cast-on edge, ending with a p row.

TO SHAPE NECK

• **Next row**: K49 (51:53) sts, turn and work on these sts for first side of neck.
• Dec 1 st at neck edge on next and 2 foll alt rows.
• Work 1 row.
• Change to size 6 (4mm) needles.
• Cont in seed st, at the same time cont to dec on every foll alt row until 40 (42:44) sts rem.
• Cont straight until front measures same as back to shoulder, ending at side edge.

TO SHAPE SHOULDER

• Bind off 20 (21:22) sts at beg of next row.
• Work 1 row.
• Bind off rem 20 (21:22) sts.
• With right side facing, slip center 23 (25:27) sts onto a holder, rejoin yarn to rem sts, k to end.
• Complete to match first side.

Sleeves

• With size 7 (4.5mm) needles, cast on 40 (42:44) sts.
• Beg with a k row, cont in st st for 6 rows.
• **Next row (inc row)**: K3, m1, k to last 3 sts, m1, k3.
• Work 3 rows.

- Rep the last 4 rows until there are 92 (94:96) sts.
- Work straight until sleeve measures 18¾ (19¼:19½) inches/48 (49:50) cm from cast-on edge, ending with a p row.
- Bind off.

Pocket

- With size 7 (4.5 mm) needles, cast on 29 (31:33) sts.
- Starting with a k row, work 6¼ inches (16 cm) in st st.
- Change to size 6 (4 mm) needles.
- Work ¾ inch (2 cm) in seed st.
- Bind off in seed st.

Neck band

- Join right shoulder seam.
- With size 6 (4 mm) needles and right side facing, pick up and k 16 sts down left side of front neck, k across sts from center neck, pick up and k 16 sts up right side of front neck, 6 sts down right side of back neck, 33 (35:37) sts from center neck, pick up and k 7 sts from left back neck. 101, 105, 109 sts.
- Work 2½ inches (6 cm) in seed st.
- Bind off in seed st.

Cuffs (make two)

- With size 6 (4mm) needles, cast on 13 sts.
- Work 9½ inches (24 cm) in seed st.
- **Shape end:** Dec 1 st at each end of the next and every foll alt row until 3 sts rem.
- **Next row:** Sl 1, k2 tog, psso and fasten off.

Pocket tab

- With size 6 (4 mm) needles, cast on 7 sts.
- Work 9½ inches (24 cm) in seed st.
- **Shape end:** Dec 1 st at each end of the next and foll alt row.
- Work 1 row.
- **Next row:** Sl 1, k2 tog, psso and fasten off.

To finish

- With center of sleeve to shoulder seam, sew on sleeves. Join side and sleeve seams. Sew on pocket. Lap shaped end of cuff over short end, and sew cuff to lower edge of sleeve; sew on buttons. Sew pocket tab to center of first row of seed st on wrong side, bring tab to right side, and sew in position with button.

Man's sweater with zipper

This is a variation on the Sweater with seed stitch borders. A pouch pocket has been added, as well as a hem to the bottom edge and cuffs. A zipper is used on the neckline, and knitted cord gives the appearance of cable work on the sleeves and pocket edge.

   The measurements and gauge are the same as for the Sweater with seed stitch borders.

Materials

22 (23:24) x 2 oz (50 g) balls Jaeger Matchmaker merino aran in shade 754.
1 pair each size 6 (4 mm) and size 7 (4.5 mm) needles
Set of four double-pointed size 6 (4 mm) needles
4 inch (10 cm) zipper

Back

- With size 6 (4 mm) needles, cast on 122 (128:134) sts.
- Beg with a k row, cont in st st for 15 rows.
- **Next row (fold line to form hemline)**: K to end.
- Change to size 7 (4.5 mm) needles.
- Beg with a k row, cont in st st until back measures 23 (24:24¾) inches/ 59 (61:63) cm from hemline, ending with a p row.

To shape neck

- **Next row**: k44 (46:48) sts, turn and work on these sts for first side of neck.
- Dec 1 st at neck edge on next 4 rows.
- Work 1 row.

TO SHAPE SHOULDER

- Bind off 20 (21:22) sts at beg of next row.
- Work 1 row.
- Bind off rem 20 (21:22) sts.
- With right side facing, slip next 34 (36:38) sts on a spare needle, rejoin yarn to next st, k to end.
- Complete to match first side.

Pocket lining

- With size 6 (4 mm) needles, cast on 48 (50:52) sts.
- Starting with a k row, work 16 rows in st st.
- Leave these sts on a spare needle.

Front

- With size 6 (4mm) needles, cast on 122 (128:134) sts.
- Beg with a k row, cont in st st for 15 rows.
- **Next row (fold line to make hemline)**: K to end.
- Change to size 7 (4.5 mm) needles.
- Beg with a k row, work 32 rows in st st.

PLACE POCKET

- **Next row**: K37 (39:41) sts, leave these sts on a holder, k next 48 (50:52) sts, turn and leave rem 37 (39:41) sts on a holder.
- Starting with a p row, work 45 rows on 48 (50:52) sts, leave these sts on a holder.
- With right side facing, slip sts on left-hand side of front onto a needle, k across sts of pocket lining, then k37 (39:41) sts on right-hand side of front. 122 (127:132) sts.
- Starting with a p row, work 45 rows.
- **Next row**: With right side facing k37 (39:41), with pocket lining behind front, [k next st on front tog with next st on pocket lining] 48 (50:52) times, k37 (39:41). 122 (127:132) sts.
- Starting with a p row, cont in st st until front measures 21½ (22½:23) inches/ 55 (57:59) cm from hemline, ending with a p row.

TO SHAPE NECK

- **Next row**: K49 (51:53) sts, turn and work on these sts for first side of neck.
- Dec 1 st at neck edge on every foll alt row until 40 (42:44) sts rem.
- Cont straight until front measures same as back to shoulder, ending at side edge.

TO SHAPE SHOULDER

- Bind off 20 (21:22) sts at beg of next row.
- Work 1 row.
- Bind off rem 20 (21:22) sts.
- With right side facing, slip center 24 (26:28) sts onto a holder, rejoin yarn to rem sts, k to end.
- Complete to match first side.

Sleeves

- With size 6 (4mm) needles, cast on 40 (42:44) sts.
- Beg with a k row, cont in st st for 15 rows.
- **Next row (fold line to form hemline)**: K to end.
- Change to size 7 (4.5 mm) needles.
- Beg with a k row, cont in st st.
- Work 20 rows.

- **Next row (inc row):** K3, m1, k to last 3 sts, m1, k3.
- Work 3 rows.
- Rep the last 4 rows until there are 92 (94:96) sts.
- Work straight until sleeve measures 21 (21¼:22) inches/54 (55:56) cm from hemline, ending with a p row.
- Bind off.

Neck band

- Join shoulder seams.
- With set of size 6 (4mm) double-pointed needles and right side facing, slip first 12 (13:14) sts from front neck onto a needle, join on yarn, pick up and k15 sts up right side of front neck, 8 sts down right side of back neck. K across 34 (36:38) sts from back neck, pick up and k15 sts down left side of front neck, k across first 12 (13:14) sts from front neck holder.
- Arrange sts evenly on three needles and work backward and forward in rows.
- **Next row:** K1, p to last st, k1.
- **Next row:** K to end.
- Rep the last 2 rows until neckband measures 4 inches (10 cm), ending with a rs row.
- Knit 1 row to form hemline.
- **Next row:** K1, p to last st, k1.
- **Next row:** K to end.
- Rep last 2 rows until neckband measures 4 inches (10 cm) from fold line, ending with a ws row.
- Bind off.

Cords

- **Make two:** With two double-pointed size 6 (4 mm) needles, cast on 4 sts.
K 1 row, do not turn * now bring yarn tightly across the back of the work, k4; rep from * until cord measures 39 inches (100 cm). Fasten off.
- Make two more cords 6 inches (15 cm) long.

To finish

- With center of sleeve to shoulder seam, sew on sleeves. Join side and sleeve seams. Sew down pocket lining. Sew in zipper. Pin and sew cords in place.

Index

Page numbers in *italics* refer to illustrations

A
abbreviations 15, 27
acrylic 13, 14
alpaca 12
angora 12
Aran patterns 9
"argyle" motif *15*

B
backstitch 36, 42, 79
bags 11, *11*
ball band information 14
ball winder 11
bands, attaching 40, 41
basic skills 16–26
  binding off 26
  circular knitting 25
  holding the needles 16
  how to produce a knitted fabric
    20–23
  importance of gauge 24
  key cast-ons 17–19
  the right and wrong side 23
baskets 11
basting 79
Beaded handbag 121
beading 76–77
beads 121
bias knitting 34
binding off 10, 26, 47–49
blanket stitch 67, 80
blocking 56–57
bobbins 11, *11*, 92
bobbles 30, 63, 68–69
  edging 88, 89
boucle *13*
Boy's jacket with intarsia detail
  110–111
bullion stitch 81
buttonhole stitch 80
buttons and buttonholes 62–67

C
cable 9, 19, 30, 52, 85
cable needles 9, *9*, 15
camel hair 12
care essentials *see under*
  finishing techniques
cashmere 12
cast-ons
  cable method 18–19
  chain 46
  invisible 19
  long-tail 18
  making a slipknot 17
  picot 47
  using the thumb method 17
chain stitch 80
chenille *13*, 19, 35
Child's jacket 106–107
circular knitting 25
circular needles 8, *8*, 25
collars, attaching 40, 42
color work *see under*
  finishing techniques
corners 34
cotton 12, *12*
crochet hook 10, *10*, 46, 47, 75
cross-stitch 80
cuffs 25

D
decreasing 30–31
Dorset buttons 63
double-pointed needles 25
dropped stitches 10, 82–83
drying 56–57
duplicate stitch 98
dye lots 14

E
edgings *see under* finishing techniques
Embellished cushion 104
Embroidered jacket with picot edge
  108–109
embroidery 35, 63, 79–81

equipment *see* materials
  and equipment
eyelets 53
  button hole 64–65
  edging 86
  eyelet increase 32, *32*

F
facing 54
  mitered 55
Fair Isle technique 25, 84, 94–97,
  115–117, 120
Finishing techniques 28–99
  additions
    pockets 58–60
    shoulder pads 61
    zippers 61
  buttons and buttonholes 62–67
  care essentials
    drying and blocking 56–57
    steaming and pressing 57
    washing 56
  casting on and binding off
  techniques
    binding off 47–49
    casting on 46–47
    hems 53, 55
    selvages 52
    turning rows or short-row
      shaping 50–51
    vertical hems or facings 54–55
  color work 92–99
    correcting 84
    Fair Isle 94–97, 99
    intarsia 92–93, 99
  correcting mistakes 82–85
  directory of edgings
    bobble edgings 88–89
    lace 90–91
    simple edgings 86–87
  embellishments
    beading 76–77
    bobbles 68–69
    embroidery 79–81
    fringes 74–75
    knitted cord or i-cord 72–73

    knitted flowers 74
    pom-poms 71
    sequins 78
    tassels 70
    twisted cord 73
  picking up stitches 44–45
  sewn stitches
    attaching bands and collars
      40–42
    grafting 43
    seams 35–39
  shaping techniques
    bias knitting 34
    decreasing 30–31
    fully fashioning 34
    increasing 32–33
flake *13*
flat seam 41
flowers, knitted 74
French knot 81
French method 16
French (spool) knitting 73
fringes 74–75
fully fashioning 34

G
garter stitch 22, 23, 52, 54, 87,
  88, *89*
gauge swatch 15, 24, *24*
German or continental method
  16, 21
German or double cable method 18
gimp *13*
grafting 43
graph paper 11, *11*
graph pattern *15*, 99

H
hemp 13
hems 53
  vertical hems or facings 54–55
herringbone stitch 55

I
increasing 32–33
intarsia 11, 25, 84, 92–93, 99, 110

J
jute 13

K
knit stitch 20, 21
knitted cord or i-cord 72
knitted-in bands 41
knitting spool 11, *11*

L
lace 90–91, 112–114
lace patterns 30
latch hooks 10, *10*
lazy daisy 80
left-handedness 16
linen 12, *12*
long-tail cast on 18
loop
    knitted 66
    sewn 67

M
Man's sweater with seed stitch
    borders 122–123
Man's sweater with zipper
    124–125
materials and equipment 8–15
    additional accessories 11
    buying yarn 14
    needles 8
    other essential knitting equipment
        9–10
    ply 13
    reading the pattern 15
    yarns 12
mattress stitch 37–39
mistakes, correcting 82–85
miters 34
mohair 12, 35
moss (seed) stitch 22

N
neckbands 25, 42
needle gauge 9, *9*
needle sizes 8–9, 14
needles

cable 9, *9*, 15
circular 25
double-pointed 25
holding the 16
knitting 8–9
sewing 10, *10*
notebook 11
nylon 13

O
oversewing (overcasting) 41
    buttonholes 67

P
Patchwork cushions 102–103
pattern, reading the 15
picking up stitches 44–45
picot 47, 48, 53, 87, 108
pins 10, *10*
ply 13
pockets 35, 40, 58–60, 81
point protectors 10, *10*
polyester 13, *13*
pom pom makers 11, *11*
pom-poms 71
pressing 57
projects 100–125
    Beaded handbag 121
    Boy's jacket with intarsia detail
        110–111
    Child's jacket 106–107
    Drawstring coin bag with Fair Isle
        detail 120
    Embellished cushion 104
    Embroidered jacket with picot
        edge 108–109
    Intarsia cushion 105
    Jacket with Fair Isle border
        115–117
    Man's sweater with seed stitch
        borders 122–123
    Man's sweater with zipper
        124–125
    Patchwork cushions 102–103
    Small shoulder bag with flap detail
        118–119

Woman's jacket with lacy border
    112–114
purl stitch 20, 21

R
raffia 13, *13*
raglan sleeve 34
ramie 13
rayon 13
recommended knitted gauge 14
reverse seam 39
reverse stitch 23
reverse stockinette stitch 39
rib 23
    binding off in 48
    double 23, *23*
    single 23, *23*, 39
ribbon *13*
right side 23, *23*
row counter 10, *10*
rows, unraveling 84
running stitch 79

S
satin stitch 81
scissors 10, *10*
Scottish or English method 16
scrapbook 11
seams 35–39
seed (moss) stitch 22, 122, 123
selvages 52
sequins 78
sewing in ends 35, 99
sewing needles 10, *10*
sewn stitches *see under*
    finishing techniques
shaping techniques *see under*
    finishing techniques
short-row shaping *see* turning rows
shoulder pads 61
silk 12, *12*
sisal 13
slipknot 17, 18
slipping a stitch 22
slipstitch 40, 42, 52, 54, 77
slub *13*, 19

Small shoulder bag with flap detail
    118–119
spiral *13*
spool (French) knitting 73
steaming 57
stem stitch 79
stitch holders 10, *10*, 15
stitch markers 10, *10*, 25
stockinette stitch 22, 23, 52, 78, 83
stranding 94–95
Swiss darning 98

T
tape *13*
tape measure 10, *10*
tassels 70
thumb method 17
trimmings 35
turning rows 50–51
turning the work 21
twisted cord 73

U
unraveling stitch by stitch 84

V
viscose *13*

W
washing 56
weaving 94, 96–97
whipstitch 55
Woman's jacket with Fair Isle border
    115–117
Woman's jacket with lacy border
    112–114
wool 12, *12*
wrong side 23, *23*

Y
yarn swift 11
yarns 12–14
    worsted (4-ply) 14

Z
zipper 61, 124, 125

Credits

I would like to thank **Kate Buller** and all at **Rowan Yarns** for their continued help and support, and for providing me with all their irresistible yarns and garments.

Thank you to **Tracie Lee** and **Fiona Robertson** for their editing skills and general back-up help. **Sally Bond** for her never-ending enthusiasm and artistic expertise. **Martin Norris** for his excellent photography and tea making.

Thank you to **Triscia O'Dea** and **Jackie Stanton** for helping me out with all the knitting and **Penny Hill** for the pattern writing and invaluable help with the finished projects.

Thank you to **Heather Esswood** for her lovely hands and kind words.

Thank you to **Andy**, **Charlie** and **Summer** for all their emotional support and for always being there for me when I needed them.

DEDICATION

I would like to dedicate this book to my parents, **Margaret** and **Roy**, for their relentless love and support.